6194

Denali Solo

Ed Darack

Ed Darack
Photography
Davis • California

Published by
Ed Darack Photography
Post Office Box 2091 • Davis • California • 95617 • U S A
800.355.5294
Books, Notecards, Posters, Prints, Maps, Guides, and Calendars

Printed in the United States of America
1st Printing, 1994
10 9 8 7 6 5 4 3 2 1
Library of Congress Catalogue Number 94-094043
ISBN 1-884980-80-5
6194 *Denali Solo* was created and produced by Ed Darack Photography in Davis, California

Text, Photography, and Maps by Ed Darack
Computer-generated layout and design by Ed Darack
Edited by Amy Esterle & Ed Darack
Black and white repro prints by UCD Illustration Services
Ed Darack Photography Logo, rendered from image # 2051, by Bill Schaeffer

Montani Semper Liberi

1815

Airplane under Mount Hunter

Cover and Page 3 Photograph:
Storm over Kahiltna Region; #2051

Title Page Photograph:
Mount Hunter Banner Cloud; #2375

Copyright Page Photograph:
Foraker Sunset; #2213

Contents

S outh-central Alaskan natives gave the mountain that crowns North America the name Denali, an Athabascan word meaning the *Great One*. *The Great One* is a fitting title, as Denali (also known as Mount McKinley) dominates the landscape like few other natural creations. This mountain, which stands 20,320 feet (6194 meters) above sea level, rises an incredible 19,000 feet off the low tundra where it sits, distinguishing it as the greatest geologic vertical relief of any mountain on earth. Denali is a realm of superlative proportions; the mountain is located at 63° north latitude, the northernmost 20,000 foot high peak in the world. The mountain's height, location, and close proximity to the tumultuous Gulf of Alaska make it one of the most harsh but dramatically beautiful of all the world's wild lands. Denali is a grand testament of the planet's dynamic forces.

Traveling in this realm is one of the most difficult and objectively hazardous undertakings a human can endure. Denali's hidden crevasses, steep terrain, rock fall, avalanches, and weather constantly test the survival skills of even the most seasoned mountaineers. Due to the massive scale of the region, climbers are forced to carry oppressively heavy supply loads for extended periods of time. The size of Denali is difficult to comprehend—distances are deceptively great. Expeditions on this peak can last as long as five weeks, pushing climbers' physical and mental pain thresholds beyond any previously experienced. Many climbers consider Denali the world's hardest mountain to climb.

Despite its inhospitable nature, however, Denali is revered for its surreal beauty. The landscape of this region has been shaped by the earth's most powerful natural forces, creating a realm as graceful as it is dangerous. Weather and rapidly changing lighting conditions interact with the landscape, forming otherworldly scenes. Within minutes, a whiteout can give way to a brilliant bath of sunlight on the slopes of Denali, only to be replaced once again by the blank white of an enveloping cloud. The great physical difficulties encountered while attempting to climb this mountain combined with the mesmerizing scenes found here bring a heightened sense of perception to those who travel Denali's routes.

My personal involvement with Denali began when I was a child. Intrigued by a point and number on a map, I was ultimately compelled to stand on the summit of North America's highest mountain. My first attempt to climb the peak, like my early excursions into the wild, was a voyage of discovery. Alone, more out of circumstance than choice, I learned some hard found lessons and escaped death by a frighteningly narrow margin. This first trip, although unsuccessful in terms of a summit victory, focused my vision and laid the groundwork for my second trial.

In June of 1991, I returned to south-central Alaska. Relying on the knowledge of past experiences and the lessons of revered mentors, I put every ounce of effort into completing a solo climb of Denali. To stand atop the peak, however, was not my only aim. I also wanted to capture the remarkable scenes found in this region on film. I wrote 6194 *Denali Solo* to give not only an account of my solo ascent of Denali, but to illustrate the importance of high adventure, perseverance, and struggle, and to convey the true spirit of this untamed mountain landscape.

—Ed Darack
Davis, California

Photograph Page 6:
Denali from Air; #1716
This image, taken from an airplane while flying into base camp, shows the seldom seen south west side of Denali. The West Buttress can be seen to the left of the cloud shrouded summit.

Clouds and Kahiltna Region

Photograph This Page:
Clouds and Kahiltna Region; #1999
This image, taken from the 11,000 foot level of the West Buttress, details the interaction of light and weather on the landscape. I observed this scene change dramatically over the course of two hours while I photographed its various stages of development. A storm had just passed and the sun was setting; the temperature was such that I needed to run a stove next to my camera to keep my hands warm enough to take this picture.

Photograph Page 10:
Sunrise on East Face of Mount Whitney; #1479
Mount Whitney, the highest mountain in the conterminous United States (14,495 feet above sea level), was the setting for my first "big" adventure at the age of 16. The peak can be seen set back near the top middle of the frame as the highest of a series of large rock pinnacles (aretes). I made many startling realizations in this beautiful region and have continued to return year after year. Although I have since traveled to places much higher and wilder, that first trip will always retain a place at the top of my mental list of truly great, enlightening adventures.

Chapter One

Foundations of Adventure

Sunrise on East Face of Mount Whitney

A felt covered trash can marked the beginning of my journey to climb Denali. This trash can, which sat in the corner of my room throughout my earliest years, was never much more than a lavishly adorned necessity to me. One day, however, while I was running throughout my parents' house, I accidentally kicked the can over, forcing the felt cover to slip off. What was revealed first shocked and then captivated me. Printed on the outside of the trash can was a multi-colored Mercator map of the world. As I gazed at the trash can, my excitement quickly waned to silent awe and intense curiosity. I sat down on the floor and studied the map for hours.

I had always been intrigued by the intricate maps my father had in his room. These were not maps of the entire world, but scattered regions throughout the globe. I didn't know where any of these places were, nor what I was even looking at, as their detail was too great for me at the time. When the felt cover slipped off the trash can, however, I immediately recognized what all the multi-colored shapes and letters were—a world map—a grand view of the globe, free from the jumbles of annoying lines and dots that made all my father's maps so indiscernible to me. I gazed at the giant blotch that was directly facing me—North America. I ran my fingers over the various states of Mexico and the United States of America. I stared at the East Coast and located tiny Long Island, my home. I was amazed by what I saw. I had caught glimpses of world maps at school before, but none of them had ever grabbed my interest like the map I had just discovered. For the first time in my life I understood where I was in relation to the rest of the world.

After staring at my home region for a number of minutes, I explored west across the midwest plains states, then north along the Rocky Mountains. I scanned the vast expanse of orange called Canada, then turned south and traveled along the West Coast and into the Pacific Ocean, then north once again up the western margin of the continent. I had no idea how far away any of these places were nor what they were like, but my imagination was running wild.

My trip ended as I moved north, out of Canada, and into a green projection called Alaska. It was a large area with two tails coming out from the lower side of the region (the pan handle and the Aleutian Island chain). What really caught my eye, however, was not its strange shape or northerly locale, but a point. This point, located roughly in the middle of the state, had "6194 Highest Point" written beside it. Directly above this dot was written: "Mt. McKinley". This point was one of the few markings on the map, and although relatively small, was remarkably intriguing to me. I comprehended the meaning of "Highest Point", and understood that it was named "Mt. McKinley", but was not sure of the exact relevance of the number. The mysterious "6194" took hold of my interest. I found that I immediately memorized the number, and in the following months "6194" and its location on the world map would creep into my thoughts frequently. Before long however, my discovery faded into the background noise of my five year old head as the new garbage can became just another part of my room. It would be a number of years before "6194 Highest Point" came back to the fore of my mind.

Exploration of the world's alpine regions remained a steady interest throughout the remainder of my childhood, but it was by no means my dominant passion. Although my main interests swayed from subject to subject, high mountain adventure consistently remained something that I quietly learned increasingly more about over the years. I read articles about Himalayan solo climbs and grueling polar conquests, as well as the mountain that stands 6194 meters above sea level, Denali. All of these investigations acted as mild catalysts, pushing me towards mountaineering.

———————————————|———————————————

Early in my teenage years, I moved to California, one of the most important changes of my life. My mother and I located to a town called Visalia, dead in the middle of the flat central valley, but only a few hours from the incredible Sequoia National Park. The first place I visited was the Giant Forest, one of the main attractions of this beautiful park. After an awe-inspiring trip to the largest living things on earth (the Giant Sequoia trees), I hiked to the top of Moro Rock, an impressive granite monolith that sticks out of a mountain side like a giant stubby thumb. From the top of the formation I had an unobstructed view east, to the crest of the jagged high

Sierra Nevada. The experience was numbing—I had never been so high nor had I seen mountains so impressive. I wanted to go higher.

Although I dreamed of climbing the great mountains of the world, my most important destinations now included those peaks just beyond Moro Rock. As soon as I turned sixteen I began making solo excursions into Sequoia to go climbing. I memorized all the region's mountains and their heights. During this time my entire mountain world consisted of the Sierra Nevada, the highest of which is Mount Whitney. I had once glimpsed its summit while on a climb of Sawtooth Peak in the Mineral King region of Sequoia National Park. Although unimpressive from that vantage point, its reputation stood strong. I planned for months to travel to Mount Whitney and climb to the top of the mountain.

The weeks preceding my trip slipped by quickly and I finally found myself preparing to depart. The night before I left, I packed my car with everything I thought would be essential. Getting sleep that night was difficult, as wild visions cascaded through my mind. I had only seen pictures of the great eastern escarpment of the Sierra, which rises abruptly from the floor of the arid Owens Valley. The pictures, however, were no match for what I would witness during the following days. I left at four o'clock in the morning, my body groggy but my mind wide awake and full of excitement. I was about to embark on the longest, most thrilling trip of my life to that date. I drove south on Route 99 and then went east over the Tehachapi Mountains, which brought me to the desert and Route 395.

My journey north on the famed Route 395 was a wide-eyed one for me, as it has been on each successive trip on this epic highway. I watched the mountains grow as I traveled north, the low southern Sierra gradually ramped into the deep blue of the morning sky. Traces of snow soon crept into view, an indication of the lofty altitudes of the peaks. I wondered when Mount Whitney would emerge—I had stared for so many hours at pictures of it that I knew the peak would be immediately recognizable to me. I navigated my Volkswagen Bug around the giant formations which dictated the path of the highway. To the east were huge expanses of salt flats, the Owens Lake-bed. I had read about this area, and recalled that the dry sweeps of this now barren white ground were what used to be a large lake. The lake withered, however, as streams which fed it were diverted to Los Angeles to quench the thirsts of a growing population in the San Fernando Valley. The residual salts and other evaporites are now being mined for borax and other chemical products.

Having passed the town of Olancha, I knew by referring to my map that I was only minutes from viewing Mount Whitney. I rounded one curve, then another, always contorting my head to the left to catch the first possible view. It seemed like hours or even days, but I finally turned the bend which brought the conterminous United State's highest point into sight. Tremendous gray granite peaks, starkly set against a cobalt sky, steeply rose off the floor of the Owens Valley—the scene was hypnotic.

Set back from the broad ridges and buttresses which form the girth of the peaks on either side of the deep valley, lay a series of pinnacles, the highest of which is Mt. Whitney. I had finally seen it with my own eyes. The treeless white granite of the surrounding mountains perfectly framed the summit. Pure white snow accentuated the detail of the gullies and indentations of the massif, bringing to view different climbing routes on the mountain. A slight banner of white swirled from the main summit—icy snow blown by the high winds at over 14,000 feet. I scanned down the mountain, passing through different altitude-defined ecosystems; from high alpine at the summit, through thick pine forest, down to the sage brush inhabited desert where I was driving. I was taken by the scale of the region. I viewed the entire Eastern Sierra on the grand scale by looking north from Mt. Whitney and observing the impressive line of steeply sided mountains which vaulted off the valley floor. The mountains which stood on the other side of the valley, the Inyo-White Range, presented an equally formidable barrier in terms of grade, although not quite as high (I learned later that White Mountain Peak, north of Lone Pine is almost as high as Mt. Whitney at 14,162 feet above sea level).

The Owens Valley is one of the deepest valleys in the United States. A true valley it is not, however, as a "valley" in the classical sense is formed by the erosion action of running water, referred to as fluvial erosion. Owens Valley is a geologic formation, technically termed a graben (a German word meaning grave). The bordering mountains are called horsts, German for hedge. The process that formed the Owens Valley involved the block of earth which underlies the valley floor sinking relative to the Inyo-White mountains and the Sierra Nevada, which rose (this process continues today). The planes of contact between the rising mountains and the sinking valley are called geologic faults. The fault at the margin of the Owens Valley and the Sierra Nevada is a zone of relative up-down shifting. The shear action of this fault is why the east face of the Sierra Nevada is so steep.

The great eastern escarpment of the Sierra and the Owens Valley marks the westernmost boundary of what is known as the Basin and Range Province. This region, defined by north-south trending mountains and valleys (horsts and grabens) which have enclosed water basins (water does not ultimately end up at the ocean), extends from the Sierra throughout Nevada, and into Western Utah from the top of Nevada south to Northern Arizona. The salt flats of Owens Lake are an indirect result of this enclosed basin phenomenon. Since the water never reaches the sea, all the minerals leached from the mountains by the streams which feed the lake are left behind on the lake bed after evaporation. This is what made the Bonneville Salt Flats and the countless other salt flats throughout the Basin and Range Province. During the most recent Ice Age, all of the basins in this region contained large amounts of water; some basins overflowing into others. As the Ice Age came to an end, the region's temperatures became warmer and the water in the basins began to evaporate, eventually leaving only the mineral deposits on the basin floor. Many of these basin lake beds were made famous due to their commercial wealth and unusual physical characteristics.

I thought that it would be nice to have seen what Owens Lake looked like before the Los Angeles Aqueduct; not nearly as large as it was in the Ice Age, but not nearly so bleak and dusty as it was now. As I approached the town of Lone Pine, the point at which the road to Mount Whitney Portal intersects the main highway, my thoughts shifted from geology and environmental degradation to high adventure and exploration.

I didn't stop in the little town made famous by the mountain which I was headed toward. There is one stoplight in the town, at the intersection of 395 and the Whitney Portal Road. I made the green light, turned left, and headed up the steep road toward the impressive wall of granite. The road winds through the Alabama Hills, an interesting group of rounded boulders, then makes a straight course toward the mountains. I constantly downshifted, revved the engine, and then shifted forward, felt the engine lose power, then repeated the cycle as the car climbed higher. Looking north, I gained a better view of the Inyo-White Mountains. I could see a snowcapped mountain in the distance, White Mountain Peak itself. Dead ahead of me, the Sierra grew more obscure as I began passing large ridges and moved into a deep valley. What appeared so simple and two dimensional from Route 395 was really complex and intricate. My perceptions of size and scale were greatly distorted from the highway as well. What I thought to be a small formation no larger than a house was actually larger than ten city blocks. The "small cracks" on Mount Whitney were slowly turning into thick gullies, and I was still over fifteen miles from the actual peak!

The air outside grew noticeably colder as my car slowly moved into the high country. I was no longer surrounded by a sea of sagebrush, as tall pine trees and granite now dominated my view. I rounded some switch backs and drove further into the valley. There were no signs of anybody else in the region, it was early in the season. I started noticing rocks strewn about the road, to my right was a vertical wall of granite that had apparently shed some of its material. I had to slowly maneuver in and out of large boulders scattered throughout the asphalt. I quickly realized that it was so early in the season that the road was not even being maintained.

I eventually made it out of the boulder field and into a relatively thick forest, safely out of range of any large rocks cascading down the surrounding walls of granite. Soon thereafter, I pulled into a parking lot, "Whitney Portal" a sign stated. I had made it at last—or my car had made it. The Bug's part was now over, as mine was yet to begin. The lot was empty except for an old, beat-up station wagon. After parking my car and resting for a few minutes, I walked over and introduced myself to the owner of the car who was relaxing in the sun. I was happy to find out that the guy, named Bill, was a climber as well. Bill had been in the area living out of his car and climbing in the region for over a month. For the better part of the day the two of us discussed the condition of the climbing routes on Mount Whitney and other nearby peaks. I asked him if he would like to come with me to make an attempt on the peak.

"I tried climbing Whitney last week, and there's just too much snow for me, it's waist deep only a thousand feet up and it just gets worse after that."

Although Bill didn't want to go up Mount Whitney, he offered to teach me technical roped climbing on some of the nearby rock buttresses, an offer I couldn't refuse. I had originally planned to start up Mount Whitney the day after arrival at the Portal, but decided to wait a day and learn the basics of rock climbing.

It didn't take long before the sun had set behind one of the ridges, and soon thereafter, the air grew cold and the wind became pronounced. Bill retired to the back of his station wagon and began preparing some food. I quickly realized that I had not eaten anything all day and was feeling the effects of hunger and altitude. An hour after the sun had set, the wind grew more fierce and the temperature dropped. After pondering my short term plans for a few minutes, I finished eating and settled down for a cold night.

The next morning began dramatically with high winds and a brilliant sunrise. I woke by chasing after items which I had neglected to secure the night before. I quickly learned one of the primary laws of existing in the mountains: tie things down or they will be blown away. Bill was laughing at me when I scampered back to my car in my socks, my arms loaded with clothes and stuff sacks. Just about everything but my sleeping bag was blown away. Upon arrival at camp, I questioned Bill about what I should take along with me.

"I don't have any technical gear, Bill, not even a harness" I explained.

"That's okay, I have one you can use. It may be a little large, but that's all right, we're not going to be on anything steep."

I watched as Bill pulled out what looked like a giant rat's nest of fluorescent and metallic colored gear. He carefully selected a "rack" of equipment and clipped the individual pieces of gear onto his sling, threw the rope over his shoulder, grabbed some food and drink, and motioned for me to follow him up the path.

"Its not too far off the first main switch back of the trail."

The two of us quickly and silently moved up the well worn route; Bill's silence due mainly to his demeanor, mine to the fact that I simply needed every breath to keep up with his pace! After marching for about fifteen minutes, Bill motioned to the route off the trail.

Because there was no established path, the route was basically a bush-whack. Compared to some of the bushwhacking episodes I have had since, this first real experience was not much. At the time, however, it was quite a challenge. While Bill moved effortlessly up the sheer, branch entangled mountainside, I floundered. It was an experience in frustration. Twenty scratched and bloody minutes later, we made it to the base of a huge white granite wall and we were then in the open. The warmth of direct sunlight at 8,000 feet felt great, especially after that bushwhack.

"The route we're going to climb is west of here a few hundred yards."

I followed Bill along slabs, through snow and across exposed ledges for about quarter mile until we reached a large ramp of granite which came down off the main wall. We laid the equipment down at the top of the rock and Bill carefully set the climbing anchors and rope.

"Have you ever rappelled before, Ed?"

"No."

"Well, its pretty easy, all you have to do is trust your equipment, lean back, and pay out rope as you walk backwards down the cliff. I'll set you up in a minute."

I sat quietly and watched Bill clip a bunch of fluorescent runners into some preexisting permanent bolts drilled into the rock. After doubling the rope through the loops of the runners, Bill showed me how to put a harness on. As he expected, the harness was too big, but so long as I didn't fall back-wards while rappelling, everything would be fine. After securing the harness, Bill pulled out a pair of well worn climbing shoes.

"Here, Ed, these should fit you."

I put on the ballet-like shoes (also a bit loose) and laced them as tight as possible. Bill grabbed a device called a figure eight and secured it to my harness with a special carabiner which had a locking mechanism. He then "showed me the ropes" (literally), and before I knew it, I was paying line through the figure eight and slowly (very apprehensively at first) walking down the ever steepening slope of rock.

"Okay you're doing good, lean back a little more...not too much, don't want to fall out of your harness...okay good."

By the bottom of the cliff, I was taking long, gliding steps as my hands and feet worked in harmony with one another.

"Okay I'm down!" I yelled as I landed, releasing the tension of the rope by swinging my brake arm forward.

"Now, tie in like I showed you up here, use the figure eight."

Bill was referring to a special knot which took a figure eight form and was very reliable. I double and triple checked myself, then tied an overhand "insurance" knot.

"Now, with your butt out...keeping your weight over your feet, and using your hands primarily for balance, climb up!"

As with rappelling, I was very apprehensive at first. I stood there, touching the rock at first with a hand, then a foot, then two hands, backing off each time, looking up at the seemingly blank near-vertical wall. After a few minutes of trying to figure out how to start, I felt a stiff tug on the rope.

"Don't worry, I've got you, I'll make sure you don't go more than six inches if you screw up and fall!"

"Okay."

"Just climb! You'll be amazed at how natural it is...forget any techniques you may have learned or read about. It's all natural, there's no special technique, just relax and come up."

I thought about it for a bit longer, closed my eyes for a brief moment, relaxed, and started up. Bill took in slack as I maneuvered up the rock, pinching holds with my fingers for balance, and smearing and edging my feet on nearly imperceptible features. The granite was cool to the touch, it actually felt damp. The rough texture of the rock abraded my fingertips. The sensation was numbing, my concentration was at a razor's edge. I didn't even feel the pain of my fingertips being worn down. After about fifty feet of climbing I got to a very smooth, precipitous section and tensed up.

"Just figure it out, act naturally."

After sweating for what seemed like hours, I held my breath and powered through this crux of the ascent, ending on more moderate ground which had solid holds.

I moved effortlessly up the remainder of the climb, a cool breeze helping the sweat evaporate off my body, and the high altitude sun warming my back. The two of us shook hands and I went down for another round, then another, each time becoming more proficient. It was one of the most rewarding days of my life.

As the day wound on, Bill led me to some other climbs and introduced me to bouldering, the act of climbing very short routes without any kind of protection. After a few hours of trying increasingly harder routes, the two of us walked down the trail to our cars. I was thoroughly exhausted. While on the way down I asked him once again if he would attempt Whitney with me the next day. Regrettably his answer was the same.

"Why don't you come with me on some more extended rock climbs, Ed?"

The invitation was enticing, but I remained secure on my primary goal.

"I'm telling you, there's just too much snow. It would take you a month just to climb 1,000 feet without skis or snowshoes."

Bill was referring to the fact that I was going to attempt to climb through deep snow without the aid of anything to distribute my weight over the snow surface. If the snow was anything but rock hard, I would have to "swim" through the stuff, taking a ridiculous amount of time to gain progress.

"Look, it's not that I don't trust your opinion, I just need to give it a go and see for myself...If I find out early that the situation is too grim, I'll come down and maybe we can go ahead and do some multi-pitch climbs."

"I'd like to, but I'll most likely be long gone by the time you get back."

"Okay I'll see you in the morning."

We returned to our cars and made dinner.

The next morning was not as dramatic as my first at the Portal, but it was just as beautiful. I began the day at the crack of dawn, much earlier than I was accustomed to at home. I quickly packed my things, double checking to make sure that I had everything I needed for the two to three days I planned to be up on the mountain. I packed bagels, cheese, a stove, tent, sleeping bag, and extra clothes. I made sure that my guide to the mountain was stuffed in a convenient pouch on my backpack. I was just about to set off when I realized that I had forgotten my seventeenth birthday gift; a brand new single lens reflex camera. I had used it the day before while rock climbing, and wanted to take it with me to record my adventure up Whitney. With the addition of my camera dangling around my neck, I had everything strapped to my body that I would need for the trip and headed toward the trail-head.

Just as I got within a few steps of the path, another car pulled into the Portal. I stopped to look and noticed that it was another solo traveler. I quickly got the idea of a possible collaboration. I walked over to the car and waited for the driver to emerge. I noticed a few pairs of skis in the back seat and an ice ax. I figured that he was there to do the same thing as me.

"Hi...are you here to go up Mount Whitney?" I asked the guy as he got out of his vehicle.

"Yes" he replied with a thick French accent.

"I am going also, would you like to travel together? I'm here alone."

"Yes, let me pack a few things, then we'll go."

"That sounds good." I dropped my backpack and introduced myself.

"My name is Ed, and you?"

"Pierre." We shook hands in between his packing.

"Do you not have skis, Ed?"

I felt embarrassed at this point, as I knew that I should have brought some sort of snow travel device. Pierre had what looked like a small ski shop in the back of his rented car, and when he learned that I had neither skis nor snowshoes, he offered a pair of his cross country skis to me.

"I have the skis and the poles, but no boots. If you have correct boots, you can borrow these, if you like."

I began mentally kicking myself at this point for not bringing my skis or ski boots. Before leaving for this trip I had pondered taking them, but figured it would be unnecessary. I quickly tried to fashion a way to adapt my large, lugged boots to work with the three pin bindings. There was no way with the resources at hand nor with the limited time frame I was working with.

"I'm afraid that I am not as prepared as you. I'm going to have to slog through the snow."

"That is okay. We can still travel together."

I watched as Pierre pulled out a brightly colored pair of downhill skis adapted for cross country from his trunk. The special rondonne bindings fitted to the fluorescent yellow boards allowed him to travel cross country, go uphill (with a special heel plug), and then lock down the heel and ski downhill. Pierre seemed to be a very serious climber, and I wondered what peaks he had climbed.

"What are the big mountains you have climbed?"

Busy diligently packing his gear, Pierre thought for a second.

"Oh, Mt. Blanc, Aguille du Midi, Matterhorn."

His list grew into an indiscernible mumble of French words, all of which made no sense to me. Pierre might as well have been giving me the ingredients for a French recipe. I stood there and nodded my head as if I knew where any of these mountains were, or how high or difficult they were. After a few minutes, Pierre seemed to be finished with his list. I acknowledged his achievements with an impressed smile, more out of courtesy than anything else. Then, with nonchalant grace, Pierre anchored his list with a name that drew more than a simple courtesy smile:

"...and Mount McKinley."

I glared at Pierre wide eyed.

"You've climbed Denali! Did you go all the way to the top!? What was it like!? Was it cold!? How long did it take you!? Did you use these skis!? How many people did you go with!? When did you do it!?"

In an outburst of excitement I machine gunned a barrage of youthful curiosity at poor Pierre. He stood back and looked at me as if I was crazy.

"Yes, I have climbed Denali. I did it last May, with two other climbers, and after two and a half weeks we made it to the summit, then descended, partially on skis, partially on foot." Pierre made it sound like it was no big deal at all, and finished packing. "Okay are you prepared to go?"

I nodded, we put on our packs (his loaded down with skis and what appeared to be twice the amount of gear I had), and began hiking up the trail.

Overly excited that I was actually starting this "dream" climb, my feet moved faster and faster...it wasn't long before I was a football field's length in front of Pierre. I was experiencing very premature visions of grandeur—I figured that if Pierre could climb Denali, then so could I. I decided to stand and wait for my friend by the first stream crossing, about a mile and a half up the route.

It seemed as if fifteen minutes had passed before Pierre reached where I was, now sitting on my pack drinking fresh melt water.

"How do you feel?" I asked.

Pierre glanced up and quietly muttered "fine." He didn't even stop.

I thought that his reaction was strange. I quickly scampered to my feet, pulled my pack on my sweaty back, and started after him.

I had been told a hundred times to set a slow, steady pace. I felt so good, however, I chose to ignore this rule. Once again, I passed Pierre. A quarter mile past where I had stopped, however, the trail got significantly steeper. It was not long before my legs' enthusiasm began to wane; at first slightly, then dramatically. I was on a series of switch-backs which seemed to never end. Occasionally, I would stop and look up to see if the trail was leveling out. All I would ever see, however, was the giant stitch of the route diminish into the obscure darkness of the trees. About a quarter mile past the beginning of the switch backs, I dropped my pack once again; this time due to exhaustion.

I laid with my back pressed up against my pack and stared blankly at the trees.

"This isn't so easy...This is not so easy after all."

Not three minutes had passed before Pierre came into view once again. His salutation was brief, as he passed me, traveling at a slow and steady pace. I looked up and watched as he and his pack with skis sticking straight up moved across my field of view. I could hardly hear him breathing!

I once again jumped to my feet, now slightly aching (as was my head), and lifted my pack onto my shoulders. I decided that it was time to force myself into a steady pace. I started counting, trying to synchronize my steps with the numbers. Soon, however, this boring practice faded from my mind as the pain in my legs and back took mental priority. Next I tried to keep pace with the rhythm of a very slow song. That didn't work either. I finally opted to force myself to stay about ten yards behind Pierre, who obviously had some tried and true system down to a science.

After about an hour, I saw Pierre stand still for the first time on the trip. He was at the edge of a clearing. We were surrounded by snow. I looked as far as possible and could not see where the trail came out. The two of us walked a little further and Pierre dropped his pack. I took his cue and dropped mine as well, letting out a big sigh of relief.

"Are you feeling fatigued, Ed?"

"No...not at all."

I tried to cover up my condition. The last few hundred yards had been grueling, and I felt beat under the weight of my pack. I watched as Pierre pulled a small, hand held altimeter from his pack.

"About 2,900 meters. It will be nothing but snow from now on."

Pierre took out his skis and put on what are called climbing skins, attachments for the bottom of skis that aid moving up snow covered slopes.

"The snow looks deep, Ed, are you sure you want to continue? Without skis you will have great difficulty traveling."

I looked at the snow bank; fifty yards up, I could see only the tops of small trees, and the surface was soft. I didn't know what to do.

"You'd better get out your snow pants and gaiters, at least. It's going to be quite tough for you from here on out. You should follow my tracks, but you will not be able to keep pace with me. If you get in trouble, you will be on your own."

I thought about my chances for a minute, realizing that all I had in terms of extra clothes were cotton sweat pants, like the ones I was wearing. I did not have gaiters, and two pairs of cotton sweat pants would hardly be adequate for what I would face higher. I watched as Pierre finished rigging his skis and prepared to set off. I weighed the options, periodically glancing at the snow ahead, at the ground, and then down into the incredible Owens Valley and the town of Lone Pine, a vertical mile below me.

"Pierre, I'm going to try to go for the summit."

I was hoping that the snow would be hard packed just below the surface and that the snow higher up would be so wind packed that skis would not be necessary.

"Okay I wish you luck."

Pierre started off. A few minutes later I donned my pack, took some pictures of my friend steadily moving up the snow, and set off into the snow myself. Our route led straight up the slope. At first the snow was not too deep, I had to "high step", but not too much. Only twenty-five yards up, however, I was swooshing up to my knees, and soon after to my hips. At one point I stood chest deep in snow, unable to move, and watched Pierre effortlessly glide up the ever deepening snow. Determined, I swung my arms madly in front of me in a last ditch effort to clear a way for my now soaking legs. This technique proved to be no more than a waste of energy; I lost my balance and floundered. Extremely frustrated, I tried again, and failed again.

After "swimming" for about ten minutes, I finally threw in the towel. I took off my pack, wrestled myself upright, and dragged my belongings down the trail with me. I glanced up toward Pierre one last time as he moved up and out of sight. I got to the trail and laid out in the sun to dry off and enjoyed a beautiful day.

The next thing I remembered was waking to the intense high altitude sun—my face felt hot. "Sunscreen!" was my first thought after orienting myself. I looked at my watch and noticed that I had only been out for a half hour—not enough to cause skin cancer, I thought. I shot some pictures of the surrounding area, and then balanced the camera on a rock and took some self portraits with the Owens Valley as a backdrop.

I was enjoying my new camera. I fiddled with the dials and buttons fitted onto the device, and learned what operations each performed. I had only one lens, a 50mm, and soon wished that I had a wide angle and a telephoto. There were many compositions that I wanted to make, but was limited to only a few of the ones I envisioned due to my limited lens selection. I felt a great sense of satisfaction while using my camera in the mountains. I wanted to record on film the scenes that surrounded me and bring them back home to view over and over again, to help maintain strong memories of my first Mount Whitney experience. I scanned the area for a few remaining shots and then put my camera back into its protective pouch and got ready for the descent back to the Portal.

After changing into dry clothes, I started down. At first it seemed like my descent was taking longer than the ascent. I quickly realized, however, that I could get moving quite fast. On my way down I reflected on my short journey. At first I was depressed at making such little progress on the mountain. I knew, however, that the mountain would be there much longer than I would be around to climb it. I realized what good fortune I actually had: learning to rock climb, meeting someone who had summitted Denali, and experiencing, for the first time, the highest region of the Sierra Nevada. Although I didn't fully comprehend the importance of my trip at the time, I would realize in the following years that this very short Mount Whitney climb was one of the most enlightening experiences of my life. The combination of the clear, high altitude environment, the stunning landscape, and the physical struggle of my attempt made me want to continue seeking adventure in remote, high alpine regions. I had also introduced myself to mountain photography and laid the bare rudiments for my future pursuit of capturing wild regions on film. Just as the felt cover slipping off the trash can opened a world of curiosity and wonder to me as a young child, those first few, unconcerned moments spent behind the viewfinder at my high point on the mountain planted a seed that would ultimately grow into a life-long pursuit.

As I continued my descent, I was struck with the desire to set a tremendous goal, the greatest goal of my life so far: to successfully climb Denali. I didn't know how soon I could realistically make a viable attempt, but decided that I would do it within five years. My mind drifted from Pierre's description of the mountain, to photographs and articles I had seen. I fantasized about standing on the summit of North America's highest mountain. With my head down, immersed in deep thoughts of Denali and wild Alaska, I almost didn't realize the fact that I was nearing the Portal. I lifted my head and could see the parking lot and my Volkswagen among some trees. I flashed through the remaining switch-backs and jogged down the level sections of the trail. By 11:45 a.m, I was back at my car. I rested, rehydrated, and ate, then packed my things and visited near-by Death Valley for a short desert excursion before driving home.

Photograph Page 27:
Glacier from Air; #1658
The high Alaska Range is a landscape locked in ice. Small tributary glaciers such as this one feed into large tongues of ice such as the main Kahiltna Glacier. These tributary glaciers are fed by snowfall, cirque glaciers, and jumbled, steep icefalls such as the one on the upper right of this image.

Photograph Page 28:
Moonlight on Mount Shasta; #16686
Mount Shasta is one of the most beautiful peaks of the Cascade Range. This chain of volcanic mountains extends from southern British Columbia to northern California and present formidable challenges to climbers. When the moon is full, the upper slopes can be easily seen under the stars.

1658

Glacier from Air

Chapter Two

Strengthened Convictions

Moonlight on Mount Shasta

Throughout the remainder of my high school years I pushed myself further into the world of outdoor adventure. I climbed as much as possible, started back-country skiing, and continued to hone my overall mountain sense. My goal of climbing Denali was ever present. The more I learned of this peak, the more I wanted to visit the region in person.

I intensified my conditioning by making an increased number of trips into the Sierra Nevada. I was also on the lookout for prospective partners. Most people I talked to, however, were unable to commit to such an endeavor. I decided that if I had to do it alone, I would.

One of my greatest adventures during this period was a solo climb of Mount Shasta, one of the highest mountains in California and the conterminous United States. Mount Shasta is a beautiful stratovolcano that lies at the southern end of the Cascade Range near the California-Oregon border. The Cascade mountains are a line of volcanos formed by the subduction of the Juan de Fuca plate under the North American Plate. This range has some of the most beautiful mountains in North America, and Mount Shasta is no exception. Because the mountain stands 14,162 feet above sea level and has year-round snowfields and glaciers, Mount Shasta is a good peak to get some altitude and glacier training in one sweep. I had spent a great amount of time in the Sierra Nevada and wanted to explore other mountain environments. I had read much about Mount Shasta and learned that it is a significant achievement to climb this peak. Because of its height and reputation, I had serious doubts about my potential for success. I had already been to Mount Whitney twice and had gotten whipped twice, and was concerned about my overall climbing abilities. Mount Shasta would be both a test and a learning experience.

I took some time off from my job before departing, packed my climbing boots, ice ax, backpack, and borrowed a sleeping bag from a neighbor. It didn't take long to get on the road. Nine hours after setting out, I was on the first leg of my route up the mountain, called the Avalanche Gulch Route. From the road-head at Bunny Flat, the peak looked imposing. Mount Shasta rises an impressive 7,000 feet off the volcanic plateau where it sits, and on a clear day can be seen from hundreds of miles in many directions. Because it was August, my solo trip was anything but solo. It seemed every climber interested in Mount Shasta was on the mountain the day I was. I would climb by one group, take a rest, then climb near the company of another. I spent as much time socializing as I did climbing during the first sections of the mountain.

Mount Shasta is very different than the peaks of the Sierra Nevada. From a distance, the Sierra look like a long ridge with little topographical fluctuations. A closer examination however, reveals jagged granite mountains that are totally awe-inspiring. Mount Shasta, on the other hand, looks quite distinct and impressive from a distance, but up close the mountain's features are not nearly as captivating as those of the Sierra. I camped about five hundred feet above the tree-line, amongst a group of rocks and boulders that provided a good vantage point to examine the characteristics of Mount Shasta. Soon after setting up camp, the sun set and the stars appeared—the night was incredibly clear and still. Although I was lying on sharp rocks, I fell asleep quickly.

Clear conditions remained throughout the following day. Once the sun rose over the Casaval Ridge, the air warmed and I was able to climb in nothing more than a T-shirt and shorts. One hour after leaving camp, I set foot on the first section of snow and ice on the trip. I donned my crampons for the ascent and continued my journey into the heights. I practiced different techniques of glacier travel on the ever steepening slope, trying to find one that felt natural to me. The style I was most comfortable was the "duck stance", an awkward looking technique that I continue to use. As the day progressed, a growing number of people began climbing the peak on the many different routes of the mountain. My day's goal was Helen Lake, at 10,000 feet altitude. My plan was to spend the day acclimatizing at the lake, then go for the summit the following morning. My map indicated that Helen Lake was only a short distance from my previous night's camp site. The ascent, however, was taking more time than I had projected. It took three hours from the start of the day's leg of the adventure before I was just below the lake on the steepest section of the snowfield. I planted my ice ax and advanced my feet one by one, firmly placing each foot before moving. I was at 10,000 feet and feeling the effects of the altitude, my legs burned and my pack grew heavier. I breathed more rapidly to compensate for my lack of acclimatization and was slightly light-headed. During the night at Helen Lake my body would produce more oxygen-carrying red blood cells and my lungs would develop more alveoli, tiny cells that collect and distribute oxygen molecules to the blood cells. I finally crested the last hump of steep snow and came upon a large, flat section of ice surrounded by volcanic rock. There were tents scattered throughout the area, but no lake. I climbed the final fifty yards and dropped my gear on a high rock outcrop. Curious about Helen Lake, I asked some climbers who were camped near me where this supposed lake was.

"Where is this Helen Lake?" I inquired after a brief introduction.

"Right there." A guy pointed at the large snow patch.

"Where?"

"Right there."

"That's a snowfield."

"No it's not, it's a lake."

"It's frozen" came a voice from inside the group's large tent.

"Oh, can you get water from it?"

"Yeah, but you have to boil it first, there's a lot of traffic up here, and it's the end of the season."

"Okay Thanks."

I found a level patch of ground and set up camp, then rested in the sun. The view from Helen "lake" is spectacular—to the southeast is the 10,000 foot high Mount Lassen, to the south are the Castle Spires, and to the west the setting sun casts the Trinity Alps in a series of stark silhouettes. I bedded down after the sun fell below the horizon and slept solidly.

I woke the following morning two hours before the sun rose. Anxious to start climbing, I secured gear that I would not be taking for the summit attempt with rocks and then filtered some water. I climbed slowly, with my head slumped down, periodically looking up to gauge and correct my course. I had learned by now to keep a steady pace, even when I felt like driving ahead, and forced myself into what felt like an unnaturally slow ascent.

Throughout the morning, I climbed a steep bowl that led to a narrow strip of snow on the right margin of what is called "The Heart". At the top of The Heart, at an elevation of 13,000 feet, I stood under a very foreboding set of vertical cliffs called the Red Banks. The Red Banks are a long ridge of 300 foot high cliffs comprised of Andesite. The red color of the cliffs arises from the oxidation of iron which is part of the molecular composition of the material. Many of the different variations of the south side climbing routes on Mount Shasta converge on a tiny formation on the Red Banks known as "The Window", a slot that dissects the imposing cliffs and allows a relatively secure passage to the high ground above the ridge.

When I arrived at the foot of the Red Banks, I had been steadily climbing for five hours and wanted to rest and eat lunch. I easily found the opening of The Window, but noticed rocks and boulders scattered freshly on top of the snow. Just as I took my backpack off, I heard a hiss and then a loud whir. I looked up and KLUNK! A fist sized rock grazed my scalp and knocked me off balance, followed by five more projectiles that sped out of the opening and buzzed down the steep slope. There were large spots of blood on the snow—my blood. I was momentarily fearful that I might have a concussion and sat down on top of my backpack, out of the line of fire. The bleeding eventually stopped and I got on my way, no longer worried about head injuries, but very concerned that more rocks would shoot down at me.

I scratched, crawled, and kicked my way up the narrow tube of rock and ice, utilizing for the first time the front points of my crampons in a true mountaineering situation. The feeling was exhilarating, firmly driving the two metal claws which projected from the base of my boots into hard ice. I used my right hand to plant my ice ax and my left hand to grab holds on the rock wall. By the time I got to the top of the couloir, my legs were burning, my lungs gasping, and my fingertips were a bloody mess—but I was above the Red Banks.

From the top of the Red Banks, I could see the upper slopes of the mountain, but not the actual summit of the peak. I was at the base of the aptly named Misery Hill, a portion of the mountain that lies between the Red Banks and the summit. Before continuing to the top, I sat down and scanned the region to the north of Shasta, over miles of forested volcanic land. The landscape at 13,000 feet was barren and harsh. To the west I could see Shastina, a distinct peaklet that is rarely climbed. I cached all but my most essential summit gear, and started ascending Misery Hill after a brief rest. While low on the slope, I saw one of the most interesting sights I have ever witnessed in the mountains. High on Shasta's slopes, where lichens don't even grow, a large flock of brown and orange colored butterflies emerged from behind Misery Hill and glided low over the topography, briefly surrounding me. Aided by the wind, the butterflies moved quickly and soon disappeared behind a ridge. I stopped to watch the flock and could hardly believe my eyes. I could never have imagined such a sight.

The ascent was monotonous after climbing Misery Hill. The view, however, was not. Each step higher granted a more spectacular panorama of the southern Cascade Range. I crossed a field of penitentes (a snow field that resembles stalagmites in a cave, and can be confusing to navigate through), and came to a small hill that marked the highest point on the mountain. The air periodically stunk of sulfur fumes from nearby active fumaroles. The rocks were yellow; traveling the upper reaches of Mount Shasta was like being on another planet. I slowly climbed the last of the mountain, struggling for air due to both the lack of oxygen and the strong fumes. Although I was only a few steps from being on the top, I had doubts about succeeding until the very end. Finally, at 1:30 that afternoon, I stood on the summit. The experience was indescribable. For the first time, I had climbed over 14,000 feet, one of the highest peaks in the lower forty-eight states, and had done it by myself. The clear, high air allowed for one of the most spectacular views I have ever witnessed. I stayed for thirty minutes, ate an apple, and descended. The thin air was intoxicating—I concentrated acutely on my actions so as not to make any foolish mistakes. I arrived at the top of the Red Banks forty-five minutes after starting my descent. I picked up the equipment I had left and moved down the steep cliffs (this time by an alternate route that was steeper than The Window, but did not have as much ice). By four o'clock I was back at my camp, totally exhausted. I wanted to go all the way to my car, but didn't have the strength. I pulled my sleeping bag over my head and fell unconscious. The next morning I felt great, both strong and acclimatized. I quickly packed and skittered down the snow slope to the Sierra Club hut, a luxurious mountain accommodation, and then got back on the Bunny Flat Trail which led me to my car.

After each mountain trip, I would reflect on the experience and compare it to previous ones, examining what I learned from myself, from others, and from my instincts. Each time I felt that I not only learned more about mountains and mountain travel, but also about myself. I was slowly realizing that the most important aspects of my life were not guided by books or teachers or even other people who I had great respect for, but by my own basic instincts. I realized this enlightenment only occurred when I was pushed to my mental and physical limits. In order to grow, I needed to face those barriers that I feared most—by myself—with a minimum of external gear. Only after many trips to inhospitable places did I realize the importance of these experiences. While descending Shasta, I thought about the difficulties I faced while on the mountain and the doubts I had. Mount Shasta is not the most beautiful mountain to me, it is not even a peak that I spend much time thinking about, but it was here that I created a personal philosophy on living at extremes in the mountains and in life.

I spent the remainder of the summer preparing for the university application process. Before school started, I was able to visit Mount Whitney one more time. I made it to only 13,000 feet, however, before having to descend. I was bitter about having to go back to school, I didn't want to go. A trip to Denali was still far out of the realm of possibility, but I planned to do it anyway. I collected books and magazine articles on climbing this peak and sent off my first inquiries about a solo climb of the mountain to the park service in Talkeetna, Alaska. I also collected as much gear as possible and trained whenever I could. I was never able to do enough.

I originally planned to go to Alaska the summer after my high school graduation. My senior year came and went, including a broken leg a few months before I wanted to leave for my adventure. In mid-March I was accepted at the University of California at Davis. While my desire to experience the highest point in North America increased exponentially, the possibility of going after graduation decreased just as much. There was just too much to do, too much discouragement, and too little money. I got a job working at a truck factory instead, and hated it. The job, however, was enlightening in its own right. I realized that in every aspect of my life, I had to pursue my interests with great zeal. The Denali trip was put off until the summer after my freshmen year at Davis.

1788

South Face of Denali

Photograph This Page:
South Face of Denali; #1788
The South Face of Denali is one of the most spectacular mountain faces in the world. The hardest climbing routes on Denali are found on this aspect of the peak. This particular view is from base camp, where the mountain is visible only for brief periods of time, as the area is frequently shrouded in clouds.

Photograph Page 36:
Kahiltna Region from Air; #1700
The Kahiltna region of the Alaska Range is dominated by bare rock and ice. Tremendous glaciers that issue from the high mountains of the area continually shape the landscape. Large groups of crevasses on these glaciers indicate underlying irregularities on the bedrock that these masses of ice ride over.

Chapter Three

Activation Energy

Kahiltna Region from Air

My decision to climb Denali solo was not an easy one. I had my reservations about attempting this adventure alone. Climbing this mountain, nevertheless, was a goal that I felt stronger about than any other in my life. I unsuccessfully searched for a partner until one month before I was scheduled to depart. From the start of my serious planning and training, I prepared myself for the prospect of traveling solo. If it so happened that I found a partner, things would be made easier. If I didn't find someone to come along, I would still be ready to go.

Much of the first part of my freshman year at college was spent training for Denali. I tried to get outside as much as possible and did anything I could involving mountain adventure. I skid, snow-camped, rock climbed, and gained vertical waterfall ice climbing experience.

The first quarter of my freshman year sped by, bringing the beginning of three straight weeks of vacation. My plan was to travel to my stomping grounds in the Sierra and indulge in some extended mountain training. I packed my car and left Davis, full of enthusiasm for the coming weeks of snow and ice filled adventure. The first leg of my trip would consist of practicing ice climbing in the June Lake area of the Eastern Sierra, where some of the finest alpine ice climbing routes in the state are located.

I left Davis on the twenty-second of December and drove directly to the east side. Five hours of driving brought me to the town of June Lake. A few miles further along the "loop" road, just outside of town, are the trail heads for the various climbs in the region. After pulling off to the side of the narrow road, I scanned the magnificent peaks that surrounded me. The mountains were beautifully dusted with fresh snow. I could faintly make out some of the white smears of frozen waterfall ice that I would be attempting to climb on various mountains. I would either top-rope small sections of ice, or find a partner—the latter was my preference. After driving around the loop searching through dense trees for routes, I saw a lone guy walking down the road in double plastic ice climbing boots. I pulled over and asked him some questions about the ice climbing in the region and wound up with a climbing partner.

After a short introduction, the two of us headed toward some "practice smears" near the side of the road. My partner's name was Alan, and he had been living in June Lake for the past few months, climbing both rock and ice. The two of us climbed short top-rope protected routes throughout the day and decided to attempt a long, multi-pitched climb on one of the surrounding high mountains. It wasn't long before the sun set and our stomachs grew hungry. Alan and I called it a day and ate dinner.

The fateful morning of December 23, 1989 arrived cold and still, as do most days in this part of the Sierra during winter. We woke before the sun rose and drove to a spot near where we had been the day before. Silently, the two of us packed our climbing gear and prepared to depart. I thought about taking some energy bars, but decided not to, as my pockets were crammed full of camera equipment. The two of us threw our backpacks on and marched up the crunchy, knee deep snow. Our objective was to climb a mixed rock and ice route located in a steep gully high above the road. After forty-five minutes of brisk hiking, we broke out of the trees and looked up to see the bottom of the steep route a few hundred feet above us. Climbing unroped, Alan and I ascended the ice-veneered slabs which led to the start of the main route. Climbing over such interesting terrain was wonderful. We would frequently have to whisk away snow to gain purchase with our tools on the underlying ice, and even fashioned temporary holds out of the snow to gain progress. At times I was gripped, but concentrated on keeping my edge, both literally and figuratively.

It wasn't long before Alan and I reached a slightly level ledge that sat at the mouth of the gully. I took some pictures of the beautiful east side sunrise while my partner pulled equipment from his backpack. Alan was my senior in years, so I naturally felt surprised when he asked me if I wanted to lead.

"Well, I don't know." I didn't want to seem unconfident to Alan or to myself—"Do you have a coin?" I asked, finally.

"No, let's just flip a rock."

My partner picked up a freshly deposited rock and tossed it into the air.

"Mossy side or rock side?"

"Uh...Mossy!"

The rock crunched into the snow, mossy side up—I would lead.

It took me fifteen silent minutes to prepare my equipment. I checked my harness, tied into the rope, secured non-essential gear, and made sure that my ice tools were in good shape. I had my camera in an accessible spot, but as I approached the start of the climb, I thought less about photography as the route seemed steeper and steeper the closer I came.

"Are you sure you want to lead, Ed?"

Alan sensed some apprehension in my mannerisms.

"Yeah...I can do it."

I cinched up the wrist loops attached to my ice tools, double checked my crampons, made sure that my ice pitons were easily accessible, and traversed the steep, hard snow that led to the first of the ice.

"Put an ice screw in right at the base!"

Alan yelled just as I was about to place my first piece of protection. I banged in an ice piton and clipped the rope to it. With my two ice tools planted firmly, I looked up—I knew that most of the climb was no more than seventy-five degrees, but it looked dead vertical. I was scared. With very ungraceful form, I chopped my way up the first twenty feet. The route was much more difficult than it looked from below. I could feel my legs quiver—a condition known as "sewing machine leg."

"Ed, put in more protection! Put in more protection!"

Alan could see that I was in trouble. I was on a precipitous section and did not want to let go of either of my ice tools. It wasn't long before my forearms began to burn out. I made useless, hesitant moves with my feet and arms. Ahead was a ten foot section that was eighty to ninety degrees, but just beyond was a nice ledge. I decided to charge forward.

With my teeth gritted, I planted my tools hard and kicked firmly. I was moving up the vertical section, panting and flailing. I just about hit the top when I felt a rush of adrenaline move through me. I had used so much energy that I was now taxed. My forearms burned with pain and my calves were knotted. I planted my two tools and went to aggressively kick my crampons in, but the ice was so steep I couldn't see my toes. I was so inexperienced that I couldn't "feel" my feet into position, especially not through double boots. My right crampon popped out and I instinctively bent upward throwing off my balance, and with a metallic twang followed by the sound of breaking ice, I felt my body move in slow motion, out from the vertical wall of ice and into space. After that I could hear nothing but the "whir" of my nylon pants as I accelerated down the ice.

The next sensation I encountered was hearing my Tibia and Fibula shatter as my left crampon dug firmly into the ice, holding my lower leg in place while my body flipped over and spun around. I can't remember how many more times I rolled over, but I ended up sliding upside down and backwards. I looked over to see Alan (wearing the helmet that should have been on my head), just as my skull was about to take the brunt of a collision with a jumble of jagged rocks. By some amazing miracle, I hit a small lobe of ice and was hurled into the air and over the rocks. I hit the snow at the base of the climb and left an impact crater followed by a roughly cut trench as I rolled and skidded to a stop, aided by the climbing rope.

I lay limp for thirty seconds, the intense pain of my broken leg numbed by adrenaline. I looked at Alan and he gazed back with an expression of disbelief and fearful concern.

"Stay right there, don't move!" Alan went to tie me off.

"No! Wait, lower me a bit first."

Just then I felt the pain. I ripped off my face mask and gasped for air.

"I think my leg is broken! I think I broke my leg! Alan, did you hear my leg break?!"

Alan looked at me and said nothing. As my partner paid out rope, I wallowed down fifty feet of snow to a relatively flat ledge. I don't know what was worse during those few moments, the intense pain or the feeling and sound of broken bone ends grinding together. I called to Alan that it was safe to let me off belay, and felt the rope fall slack. My backpack had a detachable neoprene back support that doubled as a seat cushion for lounging in the snow. I pulled this out and sat on it, realizing that it would be a long time before I got out of my predicament. Alan traversed the slope and got the ice pin that kept me from going the rest of the way down the mountain, and then carefully made his way to me.

"Are you all right, Ed?"

I looked up and nodded my head.

"Look, go for help Alan, I don't want to waste our precious time trying to get me out of here with just the both of us. Find one or two other people with a sled, you know, one of those kiddy-toboggans, and we'll lower me down that way, okay?"

Given the conditions, I was thinking as quickly and systematically as I could.

"Whatever you do, Alan, don't call the search and rescue team. I don't want to cause a scene."

"Look, don't worry about the type of help you get. I'll get aid for you, just sit tight and stay warm. We don't have any food, so you'll just have to brave the next few hours. I'll be back with help, hang in there."

With that, Alan began his descent. I watched him for as long as I could before he disappeared. With my eyes clinched shut with pain, I laid back in the snow, trying to fend off the throbbing agony. I watched as my lower leg swelled to twice its normal size, a sign of internal bleeding. It wasn't long before the adrenaline wore off and I fell into hypovolemic shock.

I looked at my watch shortly after Alan had left. It was 9:15 a.m. I knew that the coming hours would not be easy ones; I spent much of my mental energy preparing for the coming trauma I knew I would endure to get down to safety. Since we were climbing a north face in winter, sunlight would never strike my perch. In a few hours the conditions would just get colder.

I kept a constant eye on June Lake's one road, which looped just below the mountain I was on. About three hours after the fall, I saw the first of what would be many emergency vehicles arriving. It wasn't long before there was a crowd of rescuers and a parking lot jammed full of sheriff's cars, fire engines, and ambulances. Although embarrassed, I felt relieved by the arrival of help, as the pain in my leg grew by the minute. I took my brightly colored rope and threw it above me to an open slope to help guide the rescue team. All I could do was wait and try to stay warm.

About an hour after I first noticed the emergency vehicles, I saw a guy clad in a red jacket quickly moving toward me.

"Hello!", I yelled at him.

I heard no answer. I yelled at the guy once again, but could only hear him loudly breathing. He did not sound back to me. I figured that he knew where I was, but nothing was guaranteed, so I yelled again.

"Hi there!" came the response.

He maneuvered around a large rock and over to my location.

"My name is Tom, you must be Ed."

"Yeah, it's good to see you."

"Okay, the rest of the guys will be here soon, so sit tight while I examine you."

Tom got on his radio and specified our location. We briefly discussed the situation and he checked me out, confirming what I thought had happened—a spiral fracture of the Tibia and Fibula. I knew that it would not be fun getting down to the hospital. During the next few hours, other members of the team filed in, and I was loaded into a rescue sled. The team picked up my gear and lowered me over the icy cliffs that Alan and I swiftly and easily climbed unroped just hours before. My watch read 6:00 p.m. It was getting dark and the temperature was falling dramatically.

The rescue team members worked with efficiency and care, and I was very grateful for this. There were slight mishaps, however, as every so often my leg would get jammed on a branch or a rock as I was being lowered. The subsequent grinding of the bone ends was unbearable. I was lowered down overhangs and pulled through snow, and with every minute my coherence waned. By 8:00 p.m. I was in the ambulance, breathing a sigh of relief, and barely conscious. Fifteen minutes later I was in the hospital at Mammoth Lakes, being fed and relieved of pain.

I was let out of the hospital the next day. Alan drove my car to the waiting room and the two of us went back to his apartment. After fueling my car and bidding farewell to my partner, I set out to my mother's, six hours away in Los Angeles. I laid my casted left leg off to the side, and operated the clutch by hand using an ice ax. My right leg did the usual gas and break operation. Driving my car this way was awkward. I also had quite a bit of sensory dulling drugs in my system. I'm lucky that I didn't get pulled over. The trip to my mother's was the longest six hours of my life; the only food I had in me was grapefruit, and that was vomited out the window just outside Bishop. The date was December twenty-fourth, Christmas Eve, and there was quite a bit of traffic. I managed to maneuver through the obstacles of city driving, and finally arrived at my destination, completely exhausted.

Needless to say, my Denali plans were put on hold. The hell of physical recovery dominated the next few months of my life. Slowly my spirits rose, however, and I pushed hard for fast improvement. To expedite my recovery, I put my left leg to as much use as possible during this painful period. Four weeks before I was scheduled to have my cast removed, I hacked it off with an ice ax on the floor of my dorm room, and began walking on it without crutches. This shocked my doctor, but he was pleased that I was healing so quickly. By the end of my school's winter quarter, I decided to go ahead with my original plans and go to Alaska to attempt Denali.

The months of April and May, 1990, were spent doing the final preparations for my big adventure. I garnered used and new equipment, including clothing, climbing gear, and automotive parts. One of the most important items I acquired was the famous Bradford Washburn map of Denali. I studied and memorized every contour of my intended route, the West Buttress. I arranged to fly onto the mountain with Doug Geeting, one of four glacier pilots in the small Alaskan bush town of Talkeetna, and secured my climbing permit with the Park Service. I used the final savings from my previous summer's job, on twenty rolls of film, and got cash for gas and travel expenses. I purchased three boxes of noodles and various other non-perishable, lightweight food items, and tightly packed everything. By late May, I had everything taken care of except final papers and examinations.

Just before my departure date of June seventh, I received a postcard from Doug Geeting stating that everything was set to go as planned although the snow conditions at base camp were rapidly deteriorating due to volcanic ash laid down the previous year by an eruption of Mount Redoubt on the Alaskan Peninsula. The note nonchalantly informed me that I could be landed at base camp at 7,200 feet elevation, but being flown off was another story. One possibility was that the Park Service would allow an emergency strip at the 9,600 foot level, further up the route. The other, more bleak possibility was that I would have to walk out the thirty-nine mile long Kahiltna Glacier into one of the mining communities in the Peters Hills. I didn't care either way, I just wanted to get on the mountain and climb.

The seventh of June finally came, and I got up early to study for my last final, which was on the subject of Chemistry. When the time came for me to take the examination, I was so filled with anxiety that I was hardly able to concentrate on the chemical formulas and mathematical equations at hand. I finished early and hoped that my grade would be good. After returning from my last final, I ate dinner and wished my friends a good summer. I was more scared at this time than any other during my preparation for the trip. I almost didn't go. Starting out on this journey was more difficult than I ever imagined. I thought about a concept known as activation energy. This is something that I was just tested on in my Chemistry course. Activation energy is the amount of energy necessary to start a reaction, and is a short burst of a high level of power. Once this energy is put into a system, the reaction runs on its own. Overcoming my fears and apprehensions of starting my car and driving the first miles on the highway toward my unseen destination required an immense amount of personal strength, a sort of activation energy in its own rite. As I drove away, I felt a deep sense of loneliness, but also hope and enthusiasm—I was beginning one of the greatest adventures of my life. After about five miles of highway were behind me, my fears lessened, and I relaxed in the seat of my Volkswagen as I sped toward Alaska.

1749

Clouds Shrouding Summit of Mount Crosson

Photograph This Page:
Clouds Shrouding Summit of Mount Crosson; #1749
This image displays the dynamic nature of the weather found in the Alaska Range. Clouds frequently envelop Denali and surrounding peaks, such as Mount Crosson, a beautifully glaciated mountain that rises steeply off the Kahiltna Glacier.

Photograph Page 45:
Crevasse Field and Ridge; #1901
As tributary glaciers merge with larger, main glaciers, the subsequent buckling and contorting of the ice causes the upper portion of the glacier to form large cracks called crevasses. These and other mountain features such as ridges and cornices are accentuated by the low light of the rising or setting sun.

1901   *Crevasse Field and Ridge*

Chapter Four

Northward Journey

1647

Susitna River from Air

Once outside Davis, I followed Interstate 5 straight to the Canadian border, and then continued on to Canada Highway 1 for about one hundred miles. I then connected with Route 97 until I reached the famed Alaska Highway. As I drove out of the confines of my college, I wondered what the north would be like. The sun had just set, and I was wide awake and excited—I felt as if I could drive all the way to Alaska in one shot.

The drive up Interstate 5 was relaxing. I had already been awake for twelve hours and would drive for as many more as I could possibly stand. The monotony of driving actually helped the hours slip by. I kept awake, listening to music and trying to imagine what my first glimpse of Denali would be like.

I passed Mount Rainier just as the first of the day's light appeared. It was a beautiful sight, the gigantic cone silhouetted against the brightly illuminated atmosphere. Mount Rainier is often climbed by aspiring Denali climbers as a practice peak—at over 14,000 feet above sea level and heavily glaciated, it is the mountain most similar to Denali in the lower forty-eight states. Many of North America's best mountaineers guide and regularly train on this volcano, the highest of the Cascade Range. It is a relatively accessible peak, offering challenges that equal those of many of the other great mountain ranges found throughout the world. Although I had often dreamed of venturing onto this mountain in the years preceding my big trip north, this was the first time I had glimpsed it with my own eyes.

As the light fell more intensely onto the landscape, I could feel that I was getting closer to the north. Dry, brown fields that I had seen in the past were replaced by brilliant green lands and open blue sky. Although I was heading into my twenty-fourth hour without sleep, I was as excited as ever. This new landscape got me thinking more and more about Canada. My preconceived image of this country was of lush green meadows and rolling hills, bordered by unpopulated, untouched mountains. The closer I got to the border, the more the surrounding landscape resembled my vision of the region. With the exception of clear-cuts (sometimes an overwhelming amount of clear-cuts), the northern part of Washington appeared very pristine. Once out of the metropolitan region of Seattle, this state becomes more rustic, traveling north.

Not wanting to go all the way into Vancouver, British Columbia (the largest city on the west coast of Canada), I exited Interstate 5 near Bellingham and took a back road to the Canadian border. I had never been to a foreign country before, and was nervous. Before rolling into the customs facility, I made sure all of my relevant papers were in order. I had been awake for nearly thirty hours and felt a bit fidgety. I entered the customs office for what I thought would be a quick and routine check. It was, until the agent questioned me about the amount of money I was carrying.

"Oh, about three hundred dollars."

"Can you count it out for me please."

"Sure." I counted out two hundred eighty eight dollars.

"Do you have any credit cards?"

"No."

"I'm sorry, but you're being denied entry into Canada."

"What!" I stood in disbelief.

"If you want to go all the way to Alaska, you must have at least five hundred Canadian dollars. You only have roughly three hundred fifty Canadian."

The agent handed me a dismissal form which I stuffed into my pocket. I was in a beleaguered state of mind as it was, and this pitfall further complicated matters for me. As I drove back into the United States, I ran down my options, the most dire of which included going back to Davis to get money from my bank. Not knowing what to do, I drove to Bellingham and tried my ATM card at the first bank I could find. The result of that attempt was the same as the result of all the rest of the banks I found in the town, "Unable to Process Request." I pulled into a shopping mall parking lot and contemplated what to do next.

After getting a very cold shoulder at the local Western Union, I went into a bank and discovered that I could get money wired from my bank to one in Bellingham. After a few hours of waiting, I had three hundred extra dollars in cash, the remainder of my bank account. I was bound for Canada once again. Now that I had a total of almost six hundred U.S. dollars in cash, I confidently reentered the customs office and breezed through. I thought about resting inside the border, but decided to continue onward.

Once the money incident was behind me, everything seemed to be going well. It was around noon when I left to travel further north. For the first time in my life, I was traveling in another country, and when I pulled into the town of Hope to refuel my car, I realized how good Americans have it when it comes to fuel prices, as one gallon of gas in Davis cost eighty-nine cents when I left. It cost $2.30 (U.S. dollars) in Canada! I was told that it would just get more expensive the further north I traveled. I quickly realized why I was required to carry five hundred Canadian dollars on my way through the country!

I passed through the town of Hope, then traveled north on TransCanada 1 into the dry Frazier River Valley. I was surprised to see the lush green hills and mountains change to a parched landscape of sagebrush and open earth. I didn't expect to see such a sight in Canada—but there are arid zones throughout the planet. Driving along the Frazier River is incredible. There are many sections of rapids and the road is built directly above a great deal of them.

I decided that my destination for that first span of driving would be the town of Cache Creek, where TransCanada 1 turns into the Caribou Highway 97. Upon arrival at this town, however, I was unable to fall asleep. Subsequently, at 7:00 that evening, after an hour of rest and food, I continued north. An hour later, the light began to fade, and so did I. My goal was to drive to Prince George, a little over five hours from Cache Creek. The closer I got to my destination, however, the more exhausted my condition became; at one point I found myself drifting off the road in a state of half sleep—I had to force myself to keep my eyes open! Finally, around midnight, I arrived at Prince George. I had now been awake for forty hours and had driven 1,400 miles. Upon arrival in the logging community, I parked on the side of a secondary street and threw down my sleeping bag on the road. I passed out instantly.

I awoke abruptly to my first Canadian morning. I looked up, and heard an incredibly loud horn blaring as a pair of wheels whipped by about two feet from where I was lying. I rolled out of my cocoon, packed up, and got going under a dark, overcast sky. I pulled into a nearby gas station and filled up—another twenty-five dollars gone. My destination for the day was Watson Lake, the first town inside the Yukon on the northbound Alaska Highway. Driving north on 97 brought me to the town of Chetwynd. The map indicated a shortcut route from this town to the Alaska Highway that would save one hundred miles. Five hours after leaving Prince George, I joined the Alaska Highway, not much more than a bumpy two lane asphalt road that lacks a center divider.

Initially built as a military supply route in 1942, the Alaska Highway now primarily serves as a summer tourist route and supply artery for those who live in towns near the road. It is the major route of the north country, yet more people travel Interstate 5 in one day than one year on the Alaska Highway. Since its construction, the road's condition has slowly improved. Originally an all-dirt road, more of the route gets paved each year.

I traveled over gently rolling hills which overlooked vast stretches of untouched boreal forest. The views were magnificent, accentuated by the low, warm rays of the late afternoon sun. The overcast skies that dominated the morning were long past, replaced by open, blue sky with the exception of a large thunderhead far in the distance. I was captivated by the cloud formation and stopped to take some pictures of it. The anvil shaped cloud seemed to be holding on for dear life, as its fuel source, the sun, was dropping ever closer to the horizon.

I arrived at the town of Fort Nelson, just as the sun fell out of sight. Fort Nelson is the last outpost of any significance before reaching towns in the Yukon. I rested at a truck stop on the outskirts of town and checked the conditions of southbound cars and trucks—muddy and dirty, a sign of unpaved roads to come.

Although I was headed for the land of the midnight sun, the area I was in was only the land of midnight twilight. A few hours outside Fort Nelson, it got dark enough for headlights—I flipped them on, but didn't notice anything. I thought that lighting conditions were still too bright. Finally, after the natural light was almost indiscernible and I couldn't make out any illumination from my own car, I pulled off to the side of the road and checked my lights. Much to my dismay I found that both had been smashed out—rocks from gravel sections of the road, kicked up by oncoming cars had pelted them to destruction. I didn't want to stop for the night, and pulled into the first available "service station" many miles further. I found a small house with one gas pump and what appeared to be a basic garage. The sign out front read "open". I shut off the car and searched for an attendant. Nobody was around, but as soon as I got out of my car, a dog ran up and sniffed me. He checked me out and then ran off barking. It was hard to determine whether anyone was home. It seemed that nobody was around, although the door to the service garage was wide open and the light was on. I walked inside the structure and called out for someone's attention; no reply. Just as I was coming out of the garage I heard a voice pipe up.

"What do you want?"

I looked up to see a balding guy, barefoot and in a bathrobe. In his hands he had a twelve gauge double barreled shotgun.

"Aah, the sign said 'open', and I need a headlight, do you have one that would fit?"

I spoke nervously, wondering why the man had a shotgun. The attendant set down his armament and examined my cracked headlights. Realizing that I wasn't there to steal something from him and wasn't a wild animal, the guy replied.

"Yeah, I'll be right out."

He quickly reappeared with what I needed, and charged a premium for the goods. I wondered why the owner was wearing a robe, for the sun had just set and I didn't think that anybody could have been asleep. A glance at my watch, however, reminded me that I was nearly at 60° north latitude, it just after midnight!

I sped into the Yukon a few hours later. I arrived at Watson Lake at 4:30 a.m. and bedded down. After long stretches of sleepless driving, I always fall quickly and deeply into sleep. My stay on the side of the road in Watson Lake was no exception. I woke and moved onward along the Alaska Highway. Although the road is relatively untrammeled, the highway does see some traffic, primarily in the form of large recreational vehicles. As the Alaska Highway wound through Yukon mountain ranges, I was continuously forced to "RV hop". I found that the vehicles traveled in packs; I would go for tens of miles without spotting another automobile, and then run into a battalion of rolling white houses.

I passed through the town of Whitehorse, the capitol of the Yukon, and refueled. The day was growing old and gray skies darkened the region. Once out of town, I felt as if I had the whole Alaska Highway to myself; I drove for hours and saw only three other cars. I noted on my map that I was approaching one of Canada's most coveted National Parks, Kluane. I passed through the town of Haines Junction and was taken by the rugged peaks to the south.

"Kluane National Park: Home to the greatest non-polar ice fields in the world" a sign proclaimed.

I stopped at a roadside exhibit explaining this fascinating corner of the globe.

"Behind these front ranges...lie the largest accumulation of ice outside Antarctica and Greenland in the world...centered on Mount Logan, Canada's highest peak and North America's second highest."

I looked toward the front ranges, but could only see one significantly glaciated peak (Mount Kennedy). I wondered what it was like beyond the first range of mountains. My appetite was wet. I was discovering new, wonderful worlds by traveling to Alaska.

I spent some time resting my aching rear end before getting back into my car. As the weather darkened, distant mountains became shrouded in mist and I could see rain falling on isolated places surrounding me. I was in a region that was foreboding, but wildly beautiful—the fact that I couldn't see these giant glaciers from the road where they were so reverently written about added a flair of mystery. I could have driven right by the place and never have known what was back there. This was one more spot where I knew I had to explore. I passed by Kluane Lake, and almost got blown in, car and all, while crossing the bridge over the Slims River. The Slims River Valley was created by the Kaskawulsh Glacier, a massive 120 mile long tongue of ice, originating on the slopes of Logan. The terminus of this glacier is hidden behind a bend in the valley, and I wished I could see it. The winds which almost ended my trip in a very cold, wet way were created by the cooling, sinking air of the hidden mountain range, funneled through the Slims River Valley, and blasted out over Kluane Lake—itself a product of the

Kaskawulsh glacier.

I felt small as the road wound up against the front ranges. I stopped for gas at a town called Destruction Bay, my last gas before entering Alaska only four hours away. My excitement was growing, and it showed. I jumped in my car after paying, and blazed out of the station. I watched rain clouds light up in various shades of red and pink as the northern sun set slowly on the horizon. I looked out toward the front ranges of Kluane to see one of the most unreal spectacles of light I had ever witnessed; with a backdrop of lush mountains and a foreground of tall, green trees, a pink double rainbow formed. The color was as vibrant as I have ever seen. I stopped my car in the middle of the road and took some pictures. The intensity of the rainbow grew with each passing minute; I felt as if I was in an arena, watching the distant storm come alive with the northern light. I wasn't exactly in it, but I wasn't separated from it either. I still hadn't gotten used to the long stretches of daylight in the north, and was once again shocked by the time—five minutes after midnight!

My excitement soon fell into a mellow state of anticipation as I jostled over the frost heaved road. I passed by a place called Snag—famed for having one of the coldest temperatures recorded on the continent, at -70° Fahrenheit. After Snag, however, there was nothing but green trees, big sky, and a thin sliver of asphalt.

I passed a sign that indicated the U.S. Customs was within fifteen miles. There wasn't another traveler on the road. My car roared on, sending waves of spray and mist off to the sides of the thin road as I hit puddles left by recent rains. I passed by Canadian Customs, and shortly thereafter, finally reached Alaska.

"Good morning" a large guy stated in a monotone voice as he came out to "greet" me.

"How you doing" I said, smiling because I finally made it.

"Any firearms?"

"No."

"Any alcohol or tobacco?"

"No."

"Carrying any exotic animals or plants?"

"No."

"Any controlled substances?"

"No."

I wondered if I would have to endure a search.

"What's your destination?"

"Talkeetna."

The agent paused and looked me over.

"Okay, you can go."

"Thanks."

I started my car and rolled off, gazing at the sign welcoming travelers to the largest state in the country. Although I had been driving for over eighteen hours, I felt a renewed sense of anticipation as I traveled the first few miles in Alaska. To the southwest was an uncountable array of tundra ponds, brilliantly lit by the low sun of the early Alaskan morning. I had never been in an area so open. Two hours after entering the state, I pulled into the town of Tok as my gas gauge was starting to fall below the empty mark. My watch read 3:00 a.m. Like my previous rest stops, I fell swiftly into deep sleep, this time next to a gas pump. Five hours after I had "crashed", I was wide awake and beginning the last leg of my drive to Talkeetna. I estimated that I would arrive at my destination at approximately 3:30 or 4:00 that afternoon.

The route took me south from Tok, towards the Wrangell Mountains. The scenery got more stunning as I moved down Route 3 toward the town of Glenallen. The only sign of civilization was the highway I was on and the small clearing on each side. A few hours after I left Tok, I caught my first glimpse of a peak higher than Mount Whitney—Mount Sanford (16,237 feet). It is a striking mountain, a fully glaciated extinct volcano, surrounded by smaller, but no less magnificent peaks. I was driving on the edge of Wrangell-St. Elias National Park, the largest National Park in the United States. It is the sister park to Kluane, separated only by the Alaska-Canada border. They were collectively chosen as a UNESCO World Heritage site, a prestigious distinction marking the recognition of an international group (the United Nations). These two parks protect some of the most expansive, untouched wilderness on the planet.

The remainder of the day took me through the Talkeetna Mountains, and the Chugach Range where I got my first close view of an Alaskan glacier, the Matanuska. I almost ran off the cliff as I hung my head out to view the jumble of cracks, blocks, blue ice, and moraines. Ominous storm clouds would occasionally allow beams of light to strike the landscape and highlight these various features.

I fueled my car for the last time in the town of Palmer and drove north on the Parks Highway, nothing more than a thin strip of asphalt cut into a dense jungle of dark green trees, shooting straight as an arrow toward Talkeetna. In the distance, the highway thinned to a thread, and disappeared as the huge expanse of forest and violent sky converged. I was in the Alaskan bush at last.

My anticipation built as I drove further north—I kept waiting to see Denali, but low clouds hid the Alaska Range from sight. During the few days following my departure from school, I had traveled an incredible distance and had gotten such little sleep that I couldn't bring myself to believe that I was actually approaching Talkeetna. Part of me thought that I would never really leave California. Another part thought that I would never leave the country even if I did leave California, and another part of me thought that my car would break down somewhere along the Alaska Highway if I got that far. Nevertheless, I pushed through, and was now only minutes from my goal. A little more than an hour after refueling, I turned off the main highway and onto the final fifteen mile stretch of road that led to my destination. I breathed a sigh of relief as I saw the first houses on the outskirts of town, and finally pulled into the airport.

I turned into a dirt parking lot and shut down my car. It was 4:15 p.m. After a short stretch, I walked into Doug Geeting's flight office.

"I'm looking for Doug Geeting."

"Yeah, that's me" came a delayed reply from a guy standing in the corner.

"What can I do for you?"

"I signed up to fly onto the Southeast Fork."

"Oh, yeah, what's your name?"

"Ed Darack."

"Ed Darack, huh."

His secretary filed through some papers and pulled out some forms.

"Yeah, we got you here for the twelfth."

It was the tenth. I had arrive two days early.

"Are you booked until then?"

"Nope...you can go whenever you feel—weather permitting that is. Nobody's flying now, you might as well relax."

"How long do you think this will last?"

"Who knows, could clear in a couple hours, or not for a couple weeks."

"Two weeks! You're kidding!"

"Oh well, you're here, might as well go and check in with the rangers."

"Where are they?"

"Down the road."

"Which road?" The people in the room started laughing.

"There's only one road in Talkeetna—the one you were on before you turned off here. Take it through town—it turns left about a half mile down where it becomes dirt. Go a quarter mile and on the left is a small log cabin—that's where the rangers are."

"Here, just follow me." A guy in his mid-twenties stepped forward.

"Yeah, follow Chip."

Doug and I talked a bit about my journey and then I left for the ranger station.

"Let's go, just follow me."

I walked after Chip. Just before I arrived at Talkeetna, a rainstorm had moved through town. The subsequent still, damp conditions were perfect for the famous Alaskan phenomenon: big swarms of mosquitoes. Both hands worked overtime to fend off masses of the "Alaskan State Bird".

"You need some bug dope."

"Huh, what? What's that?"

I wasn't paying much attention to anything.

"Bug dope—you know, you put it on to keep the bugs off."

"Oh—bug spray. I've got some in the car."

"Okay, get it on when we get to the rangers."

Chip drove out of the airport and I followed. We didn't drive for more than thirty seconds before pulling up to the ranger station. I put on some of the 'dope', and ran inside. A lone attendant greeted Chip and me.

"You're going to try a solo climb, huh?" She gave me a quick look.

"Yeah"

"He needs to get checked out, Doug's gonna fly him up soon as there's a clearing in the weather." Chip helped explained my situation.

"Okay, have you already filled out the climbing registration?"

"Yeah, sent away for it."

"What's the name of your expedition?"

I paused briefly, half embarrassed. I realized that I never took the time to think of an expedition name.

"How about Darack Solo."

"Okay, that sounds good. Here, fill out this card. You ever been on a big glacier before?"

"No."

"Ever seen a crevasse?"

"A small one."

The woman leaned a bit over the table and stared at me.

"Maybe you'd better try and hitch yourself up with another team."

"I'll think about it."

A Park Service ranger walked in as I was filling out my registration card. After talking with the attendant a bit, the ranger introduced himself to me.

"Hi, my name is Renney."

I introduced myself and the two of us shook hands.

"I understand that you intend to attempt a solo climb of the West Buttress."

"That's the plan."

"I just want to make sure that you are aware of the dangers of going solo on such a peak. The Alaska Range is like no other range in the world, with the exception of the St. Elias. The mountains are huge, the approaches long, and everything is glaciated. There are lots of huge, deep crevasses, many of which are hidden. If you're on a rope it's tough enough dealing with a crevasse fall. If you're by yourself, it's almost certain death. There are many good, easy, less dangerous peaks on the North Side, still quite an adventurous challenge. Mount Brooks would be a good one for you... no crowds, either."

"Let me think about it for a day. I'm really tired from the drive up here, and I'm not thinking that well...meanwhile, however, I'm going to stick with my original plans, so I'll finish up this card and go through any other formalities necessary to complete my pre-climb check."

After finishing the required forms, I watched a video on the mountain and then Chip and I drove to the "Latitude 62" bar, and had some food.

"Do you work for Doug Geeting?"

"Well, kind of. I'm really just floating right now. I'm going up to help manage base camp. I'll get paid a little, but most important, I'll be in a great place. I love the ride up there, anyway."

The two of us discussed my options for the coming days. Renney had dampened my hopes for Denali. I thought about joining another team, but realized that most parties would have nothing to do with someone on such short notice. Chip concurred and thought that I should go for the solo climb.

"Look, at least fly to base camp. If you feel you can do it, then you will, but if you decide that your not ready, you can just fly out. Easy as that."

I stared blankly at the wall behind the bar, still frazzled from the past days.

"Okay, I'm going to go...yeah, I'll go."

The two of us finished eating and drove back to Geeting's.

"Well, get your gear together, because if it gets even remotely clear, Geeting is going to fly. Doug's always the first up, so be prepared, just in case. I mean, if it clears just enough to get up, and you miss out because you're not prepared, you might not get another chance for days...maybe weeks."

I thanked Chip and drove to the airport. I walked to where Doug's red airplanes were parked. I still hadn't seen Denali yet; I didn't even know exactly which direction it was in. I strolled around the airplanes, partly dazed and in a state of disbelief. I was in Alaska preparing to fly onto Denali. I was so far from home and so exhausted. I had slept for only twelve hours over the last four days, always waking up to asphalt or gravel. I felt like I was in a dream. Doug Geeting strolled out as I was looking around

"Howdee."

"Hi, Doug."

"What do you say?"

"I'm tired."

Geeting didn't talk much. He had moved up from Berkeley, California in the mid-1970's to fly in the Alaskan outback and was now a famous bush pilot.

"Well, I think we can go up...yeah...let's go."

"What!?"

"You got your stuff together, don't you?"

"Um..." I tried to stall, "Yeah...I do."

"Okay, get your gear and I'll get the other two and we'll go."

There was a husband and wife team who were going up the West Rib.

I ran back to my car, wishing I could have gotten at least one night's rest before flying. If I didn't go, however, when the weather was "good", I could be stuck in Talkeetna for over a week—that much more time for the glacier to deteriorate. I haphazardly threw food into my "mule bag" and grabbed my cold weather clothing and my climbing boots. I locked my car doors and dragged my equipment to the airplane. The two other climbers were waiting by the Cessna 185.

"Where's Doug?" I asked.

"He's inside, finishing some paperwork."

I had ten twenty dollar bills crumpled in my left hand, the amount that I owed Doug. I walked over to the office just as he was leaving.

"Okay, lets go, before it socks in again."

The two of us jogged onto the runway. As we approached the prepped aircraft, I felt mixed emotions about what was about to happen. I didn't have nearly enough experience necessary for what I was about to undertake, especially alone. During the previous months I had imagined this exact moment. I thought I would be nervous and anxious. I was so exhausted by the drive, however, that I was simply too worn out to be jittery. The hundred yards to the aircraft seemed like ten miles. The other two climbers dragged their gear to the plane, just as beams of sunlight broke out of the stormy sky.

"It's definitely breaking, but who knows for how long...Hey, did you pay me for this yet?"

"What? Oh, money...here, two hundred bucks."

I handed Doug the crumpled wad of bills which he stuffed into his pocket. I was in a bizarre, inattentive state of mind.

"Okay Ed, looks like you're going in first."

I crawled into the shell of the airplane and sat in the most claustrophobic part in the craft—behind the rear seat on top of a sleeping bag.

"We're gonna hand in some stuff, help out with the positioning of it, would you?"

"Yeah, get my green bag first, would you?"

My green bag had my camera and film in it, along with basic amenities such as lip balm and sun screen. I laid the bag down between my legs where it would be safe, and received large backpacks and bags crammed with gear and food. Before long, things were so tightly packed in the tiny aircraft, I felt like a piece of a giant three dimensional jigsaw puzzle. I was amazed by the amount of equipment that could be packed into a Cessna 185. After all the gear was tied down, the husband and wife team climbed aboard. Doug secured the doors and climbed in himself. I pulled out my camera and got a few rolls of film ready for quick reloading. As Doug fastened his headset, I felt a burst of adrenaline move through my veins. All my preparations, anxieties, hopes, and fears over the past years hit me as Doug did his pre-flight check. I squeezed my eyes shut and prepared for the adventure that was about to begin.

Photograph Page 46:
Susitna River from Air; #1647
The Susitna River is a tremendous waterway that strikes across the south-central Alaskan landscape. This river, which begins at the terminus of the Susitna Glacier as meltwater and is further fed by other large rivers and creeks, is a beautiful example of a braided river. The river ends at the north end of the Cook Inlet, part of the stormy Gulf of Alaska.

Photograph Page 61:
Caribou Grazing Under Denali; #2844
The north side of Denali is an incredible realm where vast sweeps of tundra, high mountains, and aloof wildlife can all be viewed. Seen here are a small herd of Caribou grazing above the Eilson River. In the distance, Denali stands dominantly above the region. The incredible vertical relief of this mountain is illustrated in this view.

Caribou Grazing under Denali

2844

Chapter Five

Brutal Reality

[1679] *Lower Kahiltna Glacier through Cumulus*

Under the control of Doug, the 185 sputtered and then roared to life. The experienced bush pilot fine tuned the aircraft's controls and put on his voice activated headset. After logging his flight plan, Doug checked to see that the other two passengers had their seat belts secure. Because I was sitting on a rolled up sleeping bag in the back, I did not have a seat belt or a head set.

"You secure back there?" Doug yelled over the noise of the aircraft.

I made eye contact and nodded. As Doug increased throttle, the noise of the engine became deafening. Less than four days after I drove out of my college dormitory, I was rolling out onto the tarmac preparing to take off to the Alaska Range. Doug maneuvered the bright red craft down to the end of the T-shaped runway, and positioned the airplane for a south-bound takeoff. He throttled back and we stood still, while he checked the aircraft's control surfaces once again. I heard him log in something over the radio about a "one shot pass".

"Hey Doug." I yelled, "What's 'one shot pass'?"

"It's a pass...and you've got one shot to make it over."

Doug throttled up and we accelerated down the airstrip. I held my camera at the ready, with a zoom lens attached. I looked out my side window and watched the green trees streak by as the 185 rumbled and vibrated down the runway. Doug gently pulled back on the yolk and I watched the trees below grow small. To my right I could see "TALKEETNA" spelled out on the runway—we were climbing swiftly into the big Alaskan sky. Doug adjusted the fuel mixture and put the aircraft on course. I looked toward Denali—or at least where I was told it stood, and saw nothing but a mountain range of clouds. It was ironic that I would be less than ten miles from Denali in less than an hour, and still had not seen the peak. After a few minutes of flight, the aircraft leveled out, just under cloud base. Although the mountains were completely socked in, my view was breathtaking. I had never witnessed so many miles of untouched wilderness. I could see the incredible sweep of the Susitna River Valley, complete with tundra, forest, and a multitude of small lakes, split by the ever changing braided pattern of the river itself. To the south, were huge clouds dropping dense curtains of rain on the uninhabited wilderness. The tumultuous sky was randomly broken by plumes of rain and an occasional sunbeam—the whole vision was surreal.

After about ten minutes of flying, I could see the first foothills of the Alaska Range, the Dutch and Peters Hills. Doug put the airplane into a climb and we were soon encased in the gray of a dense cloud. In a situation where I should have been fearful, I felt secure. I could sense that Geeting really knew what he was doing. The sea of clouds broke apart at the boundary of the foothill's jagged mountains. I looked down to see the huge terminal moraine of the Kahiltna Glacier. I had only seen a view of its kind before in books and magazines. Observing this massive natural creation through the overcast light was frightening. Just five days prior, I was studying and taking tests on the ice age, and now I was entering it. Geeting banked the craft and we once again entered the obscure world of clouds. Periodically, we'd hit a clear spot revealing massive precipices of rock and ice, so close it seemed possible to reach out and touch the walls. These sights would quickly be replaced by white, as clouds ruled the day. I had been told that Geeting could fly into Kahiltna base blind. I watched attentively as he worked the controls with instinctive timing. I worked my camera furiously. Forty minutes into the flight, Doug throttled the engine back and the aircraft dropped into open air. Sunlight shone on a ridge of Mount Foraker, on the west side of the tremendous Kahiltna Glacier near base camp. My head was moving back and forth in a futile attempt to take in the immense landscape. The Kahiltna region is an area dominated by ice, and everywhere I looked I could see nothing but white. Doug pointed down and to the left . I could see three small dots juxtaposed on the giant glacier. The dots were climbers coming back to base camp. I wished I could see further up the gigantic river of ice. The 185 was coming toward the surface quickly and Doug made sure the aircraft's skis were down. The snowy surface of the southeast fork of the glacier raced below us as we closed in for touch down. The engine slowed to a fluttering whine and prepared for impact.

The 185 hit the snow, bounced back into the air, then once again connected with the glacier's surface. The engine roared to life under the pilot's control as soon as we came down for the second time. The fresh, wet snow slowed the airplane with amazing efficiency. With the yoke pulled all the way back to avoid nosing over, Doug powered us up the final one hundred yards to a red canvas hut where a group of climbers waited. Doug kicked the tail around with a boost of power and a sharp turn of the rudder, positioning the aircraft for a takeoff. He then shut down the engine. I secured my camera and got ready to unload the cargo.

"We're here." Our pilot stated in a very unconcerned voice. I helped send equipment forward to Doug and the other two climbers, and then took my first steps on a full-fledged Alaskan glacier. I jumped up and down on the wet snow, compacting it under my feet as a crew of emaciated, sunburnt climbers hobbled up to the plane.

"Glad to see you could make it. Didn't think we'd get out of here for days."

"Yeah, well we'd better get going, could close in any time. There's only time for one flight out."

I watched in amazement as Doug fit five guys and all their gear into the airplane. After loading my bag onto one of the sleds which the pilots fly into base camp for their clients, I pulled my gear away from the takeoff area, just in time to watch the engine crank over. Doug gunned it to get the plane moving. Everyone at base camp had their fingers crossed as the overloaded aircraft bumped its way down the deeply rutted glacier. We then watched in horror as the red plane disappeared below a rise in the glacier.

Just as it seemed the plane had crashed, the red aircraft lumbered into the air, struggling for altitude as it turned down the main Kahiltna. I reached down and scooped up some snow. The conditions of the glacier were just as described in the postcard I had received from Doug a few weeks earlier: deep ruts , pot holes, and slushy, dirty snow—it was amazing that anything besides a helicopter could take off.

After watching the dramatic "getaway", I set up camp and checked in with the base camp manager, a woman named Ann. The following day, Chip would fly up to help manage the area. The four pilots of the mountain, Dave Lee of Talkeetna Air Taxi, Hudson Air Service, K2 Aviation, and Doug Geeting, take turns hiring someone to manage base camp each year. The job of the manager is to keep base camp in good shape, groom the runway with a large wooden grader attached to the back of a snowmobile,

Corniced and Fluted Ridges at Sunset

Mount Hunter

1806

and communicate information between climbers on the mountain, pilots, and the Park Service in Talkeetna. The job requires twenty-four hour vigilance, and a lot of hard work.

I organized gear and food after pitching my tent. The break in the weather was short lived and base camp was being dusted with snow once again. Three exhausted climbers were moving slowly up the final hundred yards into camp, the three who I saw from the airplane. I sat in my tent, and sorted clothing, hardware and food. I was pathetically under-equipped. Although I had a good Gore-Tex jacket, my pants were cheap, leaky nylon, and my thermal underwear were cotton, a death material for these conditions. I had no parka, only a thin fleece jacket, and just two pair of liner socks and one pair of wool socks. My food consisted of thirty-five packets of ramen, two boxes of crackers, five pounds of cheese, eight small cans of fruit cocktail, and four cubes of military survival food.

Clouds swirled about the precipices and ice-locked ridges surrounding base camp. There was an occasional rumble to the north, rockfall on Mount Francis. The landscape was incredibly intimidating, and I began wondering why I was there at all. I flopped down on top of my dry sleeping bag, and looked at my topographical map. Conditions were calm at base camp. There was no wind, and the occasional snow soothingly puttered against the walls of my tent. Not wanting to let the inside of my tent get damp or wet, I had taken my boots off outside, and had zipped them inside my mule bag. I had a very dry, cozy "nest" inside my tent. It was easy to fall asleep.

I awoke the next morning to bright, warm sunshine. I heard the buzz of a Cessna engine reverberate between the slopes of the surrounding mountains. When I unzipped my tent, I was instantly blinded by the bright white of the glacier. I put on my sunglasses and gazed at the wild landscape as one of K2 Aviation's crafts came in for a landing. The icy, 7,000 foot vertical wall of Mount Hunter dominated the view to the east. I scanned smaller ridges and peaklets as I moved my head around to look towards the west, where Mount Foraker, the sixth highest mountain in North America (17,400 feet) stands. There were no clouds in the sky, allowing an unobstructed view of the giant mountains. Grasping the scale of the region was difficult. I studied my map and noticed that the base of Mount Foraker is three miles across. I thought I was reading the map incorrectly, but I was simply not accustomed to seeing mountains so large, and with such deceptive sizes. I examined Mount Crosson, a relatively small peak to the north of Mount Foraker, and Mount Francis, a peak to the north of base camp at the junction of the main and southeast fork of the Kahiltna Glacier.

While I looked around, I realized I hadn't yet seen the mountain I came to climb. I donned my boots and emerged from my small tent. To the northeast of base camp, between the northern ramparts of Mount Francis and an adjacent ridge, lay the tremendous bulk of the south face of Denali. I was astounded by the complex of grayish-brown granite covered by seracs, hanging glaciers, and snow fields. The long Cassin Ridge split the face in two, striking from the summit to the lower left. Although conditions at base camp were calm, I could see plumes of crystalline snow blowing from the summit in long banners. I remembered the razor sharp distinction between the granite of the Sierra and the sky above it. There was a similar, but more intense distinction between Denali and the cobalt sky above its summit. The sky was dark, almost black. I couldn't recall ever being in a place that had such clean air. Everything stood with such crystal clarity, I could easily make out detail on the most distant peaks. There wasn't a hint of haze or smog. The intense light of the high altitude sun brightly illuminated the region. The snow was intensely white, while shadows fell almost black, and the granite seemed to glow. The dense ice, which hung off the sides of steep slopes in gigantic shattered blocks, radiated soothing, sublime shades of blue and green. I felt as if I was in heaven. I must have spent two straight hours looking around at the features of the area.

It wasn't long before airplanes were flying into base camp on a regular basis. Most of the people there were waiting to leave, and by the middle of the day the camp was all but deserted. Much of the equipment that is kept at base camp throughout the season was being flown out as well. I wasn't the only one on the mountain, but I sure wasn't going to be running into many groups on my ascent either. I spent the remainder of the day photographing the area and pondering my situation. I was having serious doubts about my attempt. Accounts of the glacier's conditions by incoming climbers and Ann, were discouraging. Crevasses were "opening up" (the snow which lay on top of the large glacial cracks was quickly melting away, exposing deep crevasses), snow bridges were breaking under the weight of climbers, and the dark ash from the 1989 eruption of Mount Redoubt was becoming exposed, speeding the melting process. The overriding conclusion from Chip, Ann, other climbers, and myself was that traveling solo over this deteriorating terrain would be suicide. I would join up with another team or abandon my attempt.

I talked with two climbing parties in base camp. One was going up the very technical Cassin Ridge, and the other was bound for a Mount Foraker route. I finally called Talkeetna to find out if any other teams would be flying in. Renney informed me that a team of Russians would be arriving in a week, and in approximately two weeks some Swiss climbers, but not to count on either. My luck was out. I would stay in base camp for a few more days to photograph the area in varying lighting and weather conditions, then go down.

During the following days I enjoyed capturing the scenes of the Kahiltna Region on film. I took my fill of photographs, and skid throughout the area, becoming more daring with each excursion. I went to the intersection of the southeast fork and the main Kahiltna Glacier the day before I was to fly out, and caught glimpses of the route to 10,000 feet. I also saw the immense crevasses and weakening snow bridges that spanned them, and understood what the others were talking about. I looked out across the main Kahiltna to the base of Mount Foraker; the closer I got, the more aware of the region's scale I became. I spent about a half hour skiing around the Kahiltna Glacier before returning to base camp. As I skied back up "Heartbreak Hill" (the very last uphill stretch of travel for weary, base camp-bound climbers), I thought about my overall plans and my final decision to not climb. I was part remorseful, part relieved, but mostly enlightened by the entire experience. I decided that I would return the following year, adequately equipped and with sufficient experience to make a concerted attempt. Upon returning to base camp, I asked Ann to call Doug on the radio telephone and have him fly me out the next day.

"So soon?"

Doug wondered why I had not gone ahead with my plans.

"The glacier is in no shape to be traveling solo, or roped to a team for that matter. It's really bad."

"Okay, I'll be up tomorrow around noon."

Ann signed off and I got my things in order. If nothing else, I had seen and experienced an amazing part of the earth and would return unscathed. I watched the sun fall below Mount Crosson and retired to my sleeping bag.

Photograph Page 62:

Lower Kahiltna Glacier through Cumulus; #1679

The 39 mile long Kahiltna Galcier is one of the most striking features of the Alaska Range. It is the largest of the glaciers of this part of Alaska. It can rarely be seen in its entirety, as the mountain range is often storm-ridden. The lower reaches of this giant lobe of ice, striped by lateral and medial moraines, are exposed when summertime heat melts the overlying snow.

Photograph Page 66:

Corniced and Fluted Ridges at Sunset; #1821

The Alaska Range is host to captivating landforms at all scales. The heavily glaciated mountain range is comprised of features found few other places throughout the globe. Snow and hanging glaciers cling to all but the steepest slopes. This snow and ice has been and continues to be shaped by various forces, including wind and gravity. The resulting formations, such as cornices and snow flutes, are beautifully accentuated by the low rays of the rising or setting sun.

Photograph Page 67:

Mount Hunter; #1806

The 7,000 foot vertical wall on the northwest buttress of Mount Hunter is an incredibly awe-inspiring sight. The heavily glaciated, steep mountain dominates the view to the east of base camp and is often obscured by clouds. Occasionally, the large hanging glaciers near the top of the peak calf monstrous chunks of ice off into the abyss. These masses of ice accelerate to over 180 miles per hour in free fall and slam into the base of the peak, shaking the surrounding region and producing large clouds of avalanche debris that have been known to run all the way into base camp.

Photograph Page 72:

Crevasse Field from Air; #1718

One of the greatest objective dangers of traveling in the Alaska Range is the possibility of falling into a hidden crevasse. Large crevasse fields form as a glacier rides over irregularities on the underlying bedrock, abruptly changes grade, or merges with another glacier. The subsequent contorting and buckling of the ice produces huge, gaping slots on the upper layer of the glacier. Individual crevasses can be as wide as one hundred fifty feet and as long as three hundred yards. Fresh snowfall covers these crevasses, making travel in these regions extremely dangerous.

Chapter Six

A Second Chance

1718 *Crevasse Field from Air*

The day I was to fly out, I awoke to find two others in base camp who had come in during the night. Both were badly weather beaten—they had just been stormed off the Cassin Ridge and wanted to get back to Talkeetna. One of the climbers, Steve, was a guide on the mountain and had spent almost three months on Denali throughout the season. Mark, the other, had traveled from Telluride, Colorado to climb Denali via the Cassin Ridge, and met up with Steve after his original partner backed out. While we waited to be flown out, the three of us prepared a breakfast of nachos and eggs on the base camp stove. There was a plentiful supply of food left at the hut that was not going to be used, as base camp would be pulled out in less than ten days due to the deterioration of the glacier. Mark and I talked for a few hours while Steve slept. Ann and Chip prepared to leave as well, as a new person was going to be flown in to take care of the camp until the Park Service cleared everything out. The remaining climbers on Denali would be flown out at the 9,600 foot level, further up the route inside the park's wilderness boundary (Kahiltna Base, at the 7,200 foot level of the Southeast Fork, lies just outside this boundary). Around 11:00 in the morning, we could hear the high pitched buzz of an approaching aircraft.

"There's your ride, Ed."

I stood up, searched the air around Mount Foraker, and spotted the tiny silhouette of a 185. I still hadn't gotten used to the tremendous scale of the region. The aircraft was dwarfed by the massive southeast ridge of the peak, and although traveling in excess of 150 miles per hour, the craft seemed to barely move against the backdrop of the huge wall of snow and ice. Mark and Steve would fly out after me, as would Ann and Chip. I walked out to my gear just as the airplane bounced down the runway. I expected Doug to be landing, so I was surprised when a blue plane skidded in. The engine wound down and then fluttered to a stop. The airplane had one passenger in addition to the pilot, a guy named Darren, who was to be the new base camp manager. While Darren unloaded his things, Chip walked over and told me that this would be my ride out and gave a hand loading my gear. The airplane was owned and piloted by Dave Lee, of Talkeetna Air Taxi. After Dave and I were introduced, I went about securing my belongings. It wasn't long before I was ready to go and climbed into the front passenger seat. Dave boarded the plane and prepared to take off. I pulled my camera out of its bag and waved to Kahiltna Base as Dave kicked over the engine. We roared down the deeply rutted strip, and I wondered how long it would be before I ever saw this beautiful region again. The plane lifted off the snow and we banked down the main Kahiltna. I looked back to see Denali standing dominantly above the rest of the region. The remainder of the flight was uneventful, I barely shot a roll of film, and didn't talk much. I reflected on the short but great visit to the mountain, and wondered what I would do upon my return to Talkeetna. Since I was twenty dollars shy of being flat broke, I planned to get a job.

It wasn't long before we were out of the icy interior of the mountain range and back into the realm of green trees, grass, and tundra ponds. Dave dropped altitude and I could see the braided pattern of the Susitna River shimmering in the sunlight. Puffy white cumulus clouds floated above us and cast an array of shadows on the flat landscape below. We flew over the Parks Highway, and came in for a picture perfect landing. Dave taxied his craft over to his end of the airport (across the tarmac from Doug Geeting), and brought the plane to a stop. After unloading and taking off as many layers of clothing as possible to get comfortable, I walked over to Geeting's and got my car. My feet felt great once I got out of my mountaineering boots and into sneakers. I started my car and began pulling away just as a woman came running out of Doug's office.

"Ed Darack!..Wait...Ed!"

I stopped the car and looked over to see Doug's secretary running towards me.

"Hello?"

"You're Ed Darack, right?"

I acknowledged her, wondering what I had done.

"Well, Laura, over at Talkeetna Air Taxi, says she needs someone to help manage base camp."

"There's already someone up there, a guy named Darren."

"We need two people up there, especially at the end of the season, when everything is being pulled out, and the other guy who was supposed to go flaked out. She wants to know if you can do it."

I shut off my engine, sunk into my seat and thought about the irony of the offer.

"The job pays fifteen dollars a day plus food and a free flight." The word "free" stuck in my head.

"Okay, who do I talk to again?"

"Laura at TAT, across the runway."

I thanked the woman and drove to Dave's office, where I introduced myself to Laura.

"Okay, then, when do you want to go up?"

"Well, I just came down and...."

"How about tomorrow?"

I agreed to go up the next day. I was getting paid, and I might even be able to team up with Darren and make an attempt on the mountain. I rested for an hour before preparing my equipment and food. This time I knew a bit more about what I needed to survive. Soon after I landed, Mark and Steve flew in. Steve quickly packed his truck and drove off, while Mark stayed behind. The two of us were going to stay in Dave's cabin, connected to his office, and decided to go into town for dinner.

"Are you going to try to go up the mountain after your stint at base camp?"

"I don't know, depends on what Darren is like, and if he is willing to go with me."

"Well, it seems like he has some experience, at least from what he told me at base camp."

"We'll see."

Through the course of the evening, Mark fed me an incredible amount of mountaineering knowledge and passed on a heap of gear for me to use while on my attempt. I refused it at first, but he wouldn't let me go without it, so I obliged.

"I'll drive through Telluride on my way back to Davis and get it back to you."

Mark didn't seem to care if he ever saw the things again. He had is fill of Alaskan mountains and just wanted to get back to Colorado. After getting everything ready for the next day's return to the Kahiltna region, I threw my sleeping bag down on the floor of the cabin and fell asleep.

The morning came quickly. I was rushed by Dave to load my gear into the plane. After I pulled on my boots, I hauled my bag to Dave's plane and once again prepared to go up to Kahiltna Base.

"Ed, last minute change, you're going up with Hudson, across the tarmac."

I carried my heavy bag across the runway to a large white hanger that read "Hudson Air Service" and loaded it into an orange and white Cessna. The pilot, Jay Hudson, came out and introduced himself. He was giving a friend of his an air tour and I would be flying along. Jay ran down his pre-flight check and then we took off. I was bound for the Alaska Range once again. The weather was beautiful, sunny, with big, billowy cumulus clouds all around. Jay flew his plane along what seemed to be the same course Doug used. The hair on the back of my neck was raised high, as I could see, in full daylight, the path of our flight. Jay made the final turn up the Southeast Fork and glided into base camp. I thanked him for the safe landing, then pulled my stuff out of the cargo hold and dragged it to the place I had just left the day before. After a quick tour, Jay and his friend flew off, carrying out more of the base camp equipment. Chip and Ann had just flown out with Doug, leaving only Darren and myself at camp. The two of us discussed our post-base camp plans while I set up my tent. I found out that he too had planned to go solo up the mountain, but was willing to join forces as he was also worried about the glacier's condition. We planned to finish our job at base camp, attempt to climb Denali, then fly out at 9,600 feet.

The days at base camp sped by. Often the two of us did nothing but sit around and study the topographical map of the region. I would go on small ski tours around the area and occasionally groom the runway. It didn't do much good, as the strip was beyond repair and riding over it with the snowmobile just exacerbated the problem by making deep ruts deeper. Every evening at 5:00, we would broadcast the weather forecast, and relay any information there was to be relayed between Talkeetna and climbers on the mountain. One of the high points of our stay was talking with a group of climbers who had reached the summit. They were elated, and it was exciting talking with them. We listened to the summiteers talk with Renney, who quickly dispensed with the congratulations and began questioning them about their physiological conditions.

"Be wary of pulmonary and cerebral edema, and get down safely."

Renney had seen so many mishaps on the mountain that he was forever preaching vigilance.

During the final days of our job, Darren and I dismantled everything at base camp, hut and all. During the eighth day of our stay, all four of the flight services came in and took everything but the snowmobile and the group latrine back to Talkeetna. Even the radios were taken (one would be placed in a tent at the 9,600 foot level). Darren and I were given our last chance to be flown out at this time, as none of the pilots wanted to land on the hummocky glacier again that season. To my surprise, Dave Lee's final flight into base camp brought another lone climber, a guy named Peter. Dave told me that he was planning a solo climb and showed up in Talkeetna without any advanced notice, so he thought he might like to join Darren and me. The two of us obliged and we became a team of three. Our new rope-mate had very little mountaineering experience, but enjoyed new adventures and decided to attempt Denali. We planned to leave the following day and retired early after a healthy dinner. Resting wasn't easy that night; I was very eager to get going after being in base camp for two weeks.

The three of us awoke the next morning as the sun rose over Mount Hunter. I quickly packed everything and secured my large haul bag onto a sled, then attached my backpack to the sled with two nylon ski poles. There is so much equipment that needs to be taken on a Denali expedition that even the largest backpack is not big enough. Sleds add a tremendous amount of cargo space and are relatively easy to pull (unless the surface of the glacier is rough, as the Kahiltna was at this time of the year). As the three of us prepared to leave, we heard the sharp CRACK—CRACK—CRACK of helicopter blades. Looking out toward Mount Foraker revealed two double-rotored high altitude Chinook helicopters moving up the main valley. One banked into the Southeast Fork and came in for an impressive landing. The other continued on to the temporary ranger/medical camp at the ice bowl at the 14,200 foot level of the mountain. The large hydraulic door on the rear of the helicopter opened as soon as the craft touched down, allowing two guys to run out. One grabbed the wooden landing strip grader, the other jumped on the snowmobile, drove it down the glacier, and towed the latrine into the craft. It took only minutes for the operation. Neither of the guys said a word to Darren, Peter, or me. They just landed, did their job, and left. I later found out that it costs twelve thousand dollars an hour to operate that type of helicopter.

The three of us roped together and prepared to set out. Darren and Peter had on snow shoes, while I was on skis. It quickly became apparent that our expedition was doomed as the three of us started our descent. Due to rope tangles, falls, heavy packs, unstable sleds, and a multitude of other problems, it took us nearly four hours to make it down the quarter mile stretch onto the main Kahiltna Glacier. Once one person solved a problem, another arose with someone else. The furthest stretch we traveled without having to stop was fifty feet. The glacier was in such poor condition that no matter how we loaded our gear, our sleds would flip over, causing an immeasurable amount of grief. The situation was grim.

After three days of equipment problems, frustration, minor crevasse falls, and bickering (most of which I tried to stay out of), the three of us split apart. I personally chose risking my life, traveling the dangerous terrain by myself, over staying with my two partners. Together we made it to 8,200 feet in elevation, where the horrid conditions of the pitted, rolling, dirty glacier were replaced by an improved surface. After this point, our unified effort split into three solo expeditions. The next day, I made it to the 9,600 foot level and camped. Darren and Peter arrived the day after and Peter flew out, while Darren continued on. Darren and I slowly moved up toward the small bowl at 11,000 feet, both still determined to make a summit bid. Although we were not roped together, we were never very far from each other. As I skid up the final portion of the main Kahiltna, wisps of clouds funneled through Kahiltna Pass, at 10,320 feet. The long, spindly clouds were beautiful. I periodically stopped to watch their graceful paths; they followed the curves of the topography, rising where there was a mountain peak, and descending into valleys. I had learned about these clouds in a class on atmospheric science in college, and was now experiencing them first hand.

Upon reaching Kahiltna Pass, I cached my skis and continued toward 11,000 feet on foot. The weather was wild; clouds swirled around the region with amazing speed. One moment I would be in the warm sun, and the next I would be shivering in the shadow of a large cloud, further sapped by the biting wind. The region became more amazing with each step higher. Struggling up the steep slopes under the weight of my pack and sled, brought me to

Climbers on Main Kahiltna Glacier below Denali

new levels of concentration and pushed my pain threshold ever higher. It got to the point where every step was a challenge. I would step, rest, step, rest. My hips burned and blistered from the weight of the sled on my hip belt. It took me three hours to ascend the 1,000 feet from Kahiltna Pass to the ice bowl at 11,000 feet. It was sunny and warm when I arrived. I sat down on my backpack and scanned the rocky prominence that forms the western edge of the mountain's West Buttress (although the standard West Buttress route begins many miles away at base camp, the actual West Buttress, of which the route climbs and is named after, extends to just above the bowl at 11,000 feet). Darren arrived a few hours after I pitched camp. I descended a few hundred yards to encourage him on the last of his ascent.

Darren and I spent the night camped near each other. Due to the altitude and latitude, the 11,000 foot bowl is the first spot on the route where temperatures get considerably cold. As the sun set and the temperature quickly dropped to twenty degrees below zero, I was given my first test on how well I could solve a difficult problem in adverse conditions. In an attempt to fire up my stove to melt snow for water and food, the fuel jet jammed. In order to fix the problem, I had to take my gloves off and touch metal with my bare hands. My fingers instantly went numb, and the wind picked up, chilling them further. Before long I had the entire stove laid out before me on the snow, and was attempting to fix the problem before the conditions left my hands totally useless. The temperature was steadily dropping and I had to get the stove running, if for nothing else than to thaw out my frozen digits. I finally solved the dilemma by using my pocket knife and a needle from my sewing kit, but I could no longer feel my hands. I managed to ignite the stove and thawed out my extremities, an incredibly painful procedure.

After eating and rehydrating, I zipped myself in my "cocoon" and went to sleep. It was much more difficult warming my body at this altitude than it was at lower elevations. I awoke the next morning to high winds and drifting snow. After wrestling my boots on, I climbed outside and looked up to see the West Buttress engulfed in a sea of boiling clouds. My day's goal was to climb the headwall that leads out of the 11,000 foot bowl, called "Motorcycle Hill" and contour around Windy Corner, then camp at the ice bowl at 14,200 feet. I quickly packed and headed toward the wall, just as Darren was leaving. The two of us climbed side by side over icy crevasse lips, and up wind hardened snow. This was the steepest section of the climb thus far, and the sled made it nearly impossible to move. I almost lost my balance three times on the icy slope due to the awkwardness of my gear. I would occasionally look to the top of the rise, five hundred vertical feet from the previous night's camp site. The churning clouds would frequently fall upon Darren and me, reducing visibility to only a few feet. It took me an hour to reach the top. I sprinted the last few feet and fell over on level ground, almost releasing my pack and sled out of momentary exhaustion. In one hand I held an ice ax, in another, a ski pole Mark had loaned me. After I caught my breath and anchored my gear, I gazed toward Windy Corner. The violent conditions I saw confirmed that this feature was aptly named.

I rested until Darren made it to the top of the headwall, then continued. I fell into a trance, slowly moving upslope, constantly reminding myself to maintain a pace slightly slower than I was able. Occasionally, I would glance back to check Darren's progress. At first he was about fifty yards behind me. Through the next few hours, however, our gap increased every time I checked. Upon reaching Windy Corner, I dropped my pack and sled, and rested on the hard, windswept snow. I looked down to check on Darren, but found no sight of him. I didn't know what happened, but was nearing exhaustion and noticed the weather worsening. I worried that he fell into a crevasse, but could not recall seeing any terrain that suggested any were in the area. I felt the wind gusting progressively harder, and watched the region become dramatically more cloudy. Wisps of clouds moved around the landscape with incredible speed, and the blanket of gray was steadily dropping. I didn't want to get stuck camping at Windy Corner. I threw on my backpack and continued.

My rate of ascent decreased with every foot of altitude gained. I forced myself to continue at a steady pace. I contoured around the base of the West Buttress and jumped a number of crevasses. I was traversing a steep slope, and my sled constantly slid down and to my right. It was incredibly frustrating. Two hours after I left Windy Corner, I was traveling in a total whiteout. I followed orange marker flags left by previous expeditions, hoping that visibility would not drop further. Soon after going into the whiteout, the terrain became more level. I figured that I was nearing the ice bowl. Looking in the direction of my destination, I saw what appeared to be human figures coming toward me. I wondered if I was hallucinating, but found that there actually were people there. It was a team being brought down by a professional guide.

"Hello there!"

"Hi, you alone?"

I explained my bizarre expedition to the lead climber and then asked him how much longer it would be until I made it to the ice bowl.

"You don't have that much more to go, you're almost there."

This made me feel relieved. I told them to look out for Darren, and stood off to the side to let the group pass, then continued up the rolling terrain. I was constantly fooled by what seemed to be my destination. There would be a rise that would end with a level spot, then another rise. Each time I thought the slope would end with the ice bowl. After many of these false hopes, I finally made it. I dragged my sled to an abandoned camp site where a previous expedition had built a substantial snow wall, and prepared to camp. It was snowing hard and conditions were growing worse. I dug out the inside of the shelter and pitched my tent. I feared that a considerable amount of snow would fall and bury everything, so I put all essential items inside my tent and consolidated everything else into a neat pile directly outside my tent's door. It is amazing how easily gear can get lost during a snow storm. After rehydrating and eating, I secured everything in anticipation of a rough night. The ice bowl at 14,200 feet is one of the safest spots on the mountain to camp, as it is sheltered from high winds, has few crevasses, and the slopes surrounding the area rarely produce avalanches that run all the way across the bowl. I felt secure, but nevertheless concerned, as I was certain the storm would be brutal.

I settled into my sleeping bag after eating. Although I was warm and exhausted, the increase in altitude left me with a pounding headache that prohibited sleep. Throughout the night, I drifted in and out of consciousness, periodically slapping the walls of my tent to sluff off the collecting snow. I wasn't sure how much precipitation would fall, but it was early July, a period when storms bring massive amounts of snow to the region. It was not unheard of for five or ten feet to fall within a twenty-four hour period.

Summertime in the Alaska Range brings twenty-four hours of light. Although the sun does fall below the horizon for a short period of the day, even the darkest hours are illuminated by twilight. This constant state of lighting allows climbers to move whenever conditions permit, be it noon or midnight. This condition also makes consistent patterns of sleep difficult, if not impossible, to adhere to. I was in an extremely restless mood the next morning. I felt cramped inside my tiny tent, but the weather prohibited my exit, as it was now snowing and blowing harder than ever. I needed to go outside, however, and shovel drifted snow from my near-buried shelter. The walls of the tent were slowly caving in on each side, giving me only a tiny space to move around. After putting on all my layers of clothing, I emerged and dug out. While outside, I looked around to gauge the condition of the area and found that everything had been covered in a fresh blanket of deep snow. Visibility was very low, only around twenty-five feet, and my tracks were long since covered. If I wanted or needed to descend, I couldn't until the storm cleared. I was at the weather's whim. Although I had rested for many hours, I felt weak. The act of climbing out of my tent and standing up made me feel light-headed, I worried that I was falling into a state of lassitude, unmotivation brought on by altitude, lack of nutrition, and lack of sleep. After digging myself out, I crawled back inside my portable home. I tried not to let any snow enter, but of course didn't succeed.

During the day, I sat in my tent and stared at my Denali map. As time progressed, I increased my worrying, decreased my food and water intake, and slowly began to sink into the most depressed state of my entire trip. I no longer wanted to go for the summit, as conditions higher on Denali were undoubtedly many times worse than those where I was camped. As the storm raged on, buffeting my tent with increasingly higher winds and more snow, I decided that as soon as conditions abated, I would make a run for lower ground. I had simply had enough and wanted to descend. I prepared as much of my gear as possible for quick packing, and waited for the skies to break open.

Photograph Page 79:
Climbers on Main Kahiltna Glacier below Denali; #135
This image, taken at midnight while my partners and I made our way up the lower Kahiltna Glacier, shows the entire West Buttress as well as the terrible snow conditions encountered at lower elevations during my first attempt.

Photograph Page 84:
Ridges and Cornices at Sunset; #1993
This image, taken from the 11,000 foot level of Denali, illustrates the intricate features created by the sculpting force of the high winds over snow and ice of the region.

Chapter Seven

Climb or Die

1993

Ridges and Cornices at Sunset

The situation at my camp at the 14,200 foot level grew dire. I had been trapped inside a cloud for three straight days. Every time I stuck my head out to check the conditions, I would see nothing but a blinding, directionless world of white. I heard no sign of others around me—true, I was soloing, but the idea of not sighting another human, especially in such a storm, was driving me mad. I had one book for entertainment, which I had read four times by the end of my third day. A long duration expedition is stressful enough with a group of climbers. Stresses are tenfold when one is climbing alone. There is no one to talk to, no one to follow, and no one to pass the time with. I chose to climb alone, however, leaving only myself responsible for everything.

During the fourth day of the storm, I did nothing but sit and stare at the yellow walls of my tent's Gore-Tex laminated interior and listen to occasional avalanches rumble down the walls of the ice bowl. The smallest, most unrelated concerns intruded into my thoughts—the balance of my checking account, where I would live during the next school year, the tire pressure of my car's wheels. Sitting idle for so long pushed me into a state of anxiety. I abandoned my plans for a summit attempt and prepared to leave as soon as possible. After putting all my gear in order, I laid in wait.

My cue for exit finally came, at noon on my fifth day at the ice bowl. I noticed the subdued cast of cloud diffused light give way to bright beams of sunlight. I stuck my head outside and saw the tumultuous sky breaking apart, finally allowing the sun to illuminate the landscape. I threw on my sunglasses and packed my gear. The storm had dumped over six feet of fresh snow, burying everything. After taking my tent down, I hastily searched the area for any misplaced gear and headed out, but to where? Since I had come in during a whiteout and the storm had covered every track and marker flag, I had only a rough idea of where to descend. I took five steps, turned, scanned the area, and took five more in the other direction. I was on the correct general course, but I didn't know where the crevasses were.

Although I took precaution in consolidating my gear, I realized just a few minutes out of camp that I had not packed my crampons. I had dropped them just outside my tent, five days prior, and they were now under many feet of snow! I turned around and headed back, along my zig-zag course, and kicked through the snow to find them. I attached the crampons to my sled and ran down my checklist of equipment before heading out once again.

Driving through the waist deep snow was incredibly difficult. I would kick through the deep white powder, throw my body forward, then advance my sled. After ten minutes of travel, I noticed a small linear depression twenty yards to my left. I veered away from the obvious snow covered crevasse. Due to my exhaustion, however, I did not realize that there might be more unnoticeable "slots" in the area.

Two hundred yards out of camp, I stepped down firmly and started ahead, but the snow didn't compact. My left leg sunk down to the knee with no resistance. I instantly realized what was happening and tried to throw my weight backwards, but it was too late. I prayed that I would only fall to my waist. As my left leg sank, I could feel my right side going down as well. I looked up to watch the bright world of white disappear into a small hole the size of my body. For the first time in my life, I truly thought I was going to die. I was sure of it. So few climbers survive unroped crevasse falls. I was certain that my time had come. I looked into the darkness of the crevasse as hunks of ice pummeled my face and body on the way down, ripping my sunglasses off and burning my eyes with frigid particles of hardened snow. I bounced back and forth between the walls of the slot and just kept accelerating. I waited for the blood curdling breaking of bones and the final gasps of thin air under an avalanche of suffocating ice. I struggled to slow my fall by extending my arms, but my attempts proved worthless. I just continued to fall. Looking down, I could see nothing but darkness. I closed my eyes and waited for the final impact.

BOOM! I crashed to a halt, followed by an avalanche of ice and snow cascading on top of me. I landed on a large chunk of ice that was wedged in between the converging walls of the crevasse. I struggled to free myself from my backpack and sled, both of which were on top of me. I fought for air under the never-ending barrage of heavy, sharp ice blocks. I covered my head and face with my arms and tightly wedged myself against the walls of the thin crevasse, fearful that the block of ice I was standing on could break loose.

My first thought was to yell for help, but there wasn't anyone to hear me. I mentally sped through old stories I had read and heard about skilled climbers struggling their way to survival after taking crevasse falls. I couldn't believe that I was still alive. If I was to continue my existence, I had to stay relaxed and collect my thoughts before making another move. There was an incredible period of dead calm after the rain of ice subsided. I pulled out my camera and shot a picture looking straight up, out of the hole and into the blue sky above. It was a very rare photographic opportunity. Taking a picture soothed my nerves and I was then able to systematically plan my actions for survival.

I had fallen a good eighty feet into the crevasse. This far down, it is a constant -40° Fahrenheit. It wouldn't be long before I went into a state of hypothermia—I needed to act quickly. I left everything behind in the crevasse except for my sleeping bag and camera. I often switched from looking straight up at the blue sky, to glaring down at the small chunk of ice I was standing on. I wondered how long it would hold. After securing my gear, I attached my sleeping bag to my climbing harness, strapped my crampons onto my boots, and pulled out my ice ax. Gripping my ice ax with my right hand, and using my left hand for counter support, I started "chimneying" up the vertical slot. Because I didn't have a wrist loop, I was forced to grip the tool hard, cutting off circulation to my fingertips. I didn't care, I just wanted out. I had to climb to stay alive.

I looked down periodically to check my progress and noticed that my movement was setting off small avalanches of ice and snow, burying my gear. The ice of the crevasse was hard and my points planted well. The climbing was actually good, but terribly exhausting. I gained a firm stance by balancing on my front points and bracing my body with my mittened left hand on the opposite side of the crevasse. With my right hand, I planted my ice ax a few feet above my head, grabbed it with my left hand, and pulled my body up with both. I would then re-plant my feet and begin the process again.

As I approached the opening, the walls of the crevasse widened and were considerably softer. Within ten feet of surfacing, half my boot would penetrate the wall when I kicked. As the walls diverged, my style of ascent changed. Near the top, I made a large "X" with my body, with one leg and one arm on each wall. Five feet below the surface, I gasped for every ounce of strength and wondered if I would have the energy to climb the last few feet. I rested,

171

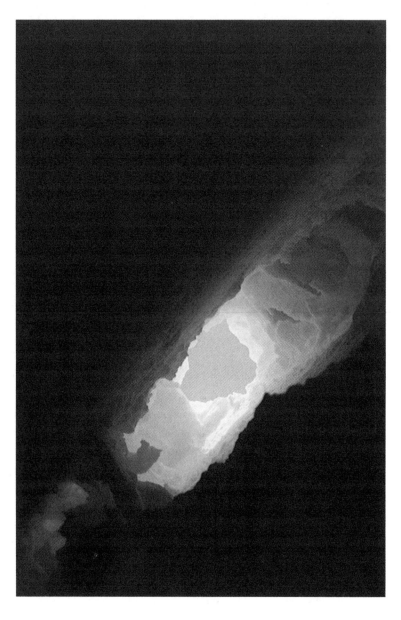

View from inside Crevasse

then bridged with two hands on one wall and two feet on the other—this is one of the most difficult maneuvers in climbing. A few more "steps" up, I found myself just below the surface. I looked up, expecting to see clear blue sky, but saw nothing but the white of the underside of a snow bridge. I had strayed three feet off course on my way out!

With no time to lose, I frantically bashed my head through the snow. After thirty seconds of drilling, I saw daylight. In a final act of adrenaline powered survival, I pulled my right arm through the snow (while still bridging with my two feet and left arm), slammed the shaft of my ice ax into solid ground, and pulled myself out of the crevasse. I crawled a few feet to where I knew I was secure, and collapsed out of exhaustion. I laid on my back for a half hour, worshipping the blue sky, the sun, the clouds, and most of all, my life. Since I had lost my sunglasses on the way down and didn't have a spare set, the intense glare of the area forced me to constantly cover my eyes. After taking a few self portraits, I dragged myself and my sleeping bag back to camp.

I knew my physical condition would quickly deteriorate if I didn't get food and water (requiring a stove). When I arrived at the ice bowl camp, I found some supplies cached by a guided expedition that was higher on the mountain. The only gear of value, however, was a tarp, rope, and some shovels and snow pickets. I knew that I needed to get my gear as soon as possible, but was too weak to go back to the crevasse. I wrapped the tarp around my sleeping bag and faded in and out of sleep throughout the night.

I dug myself out of six inches of new snow the next morning. My physical and mental condition were at a lifetime low, and continued to deteriorate. It took a shot of adrenaline to boost me out of my skimpy shelter. I was starved and dehydrated—I tried to stand, but fell over. I had to concentrate intensely, as even the mundane act of putting on my boots drained my energy. Snow fell intermittently and my tracks to the crevasse were almost completely covered. I gathered the rope, shovels, and snow pickets and walked to the edge of the crevasse. I set up a rope guide system by placing one of the shovels face-down on the edge of the crevasse, and ran the rope over the blade into the crevasse.

As soon as the system was prepared, I double checked the anchors and rappelled into the chasm. The crevasse was silent, except for the high pitched tinkle of falling ice. Once I got to the ice block, I tied off and secured my sled and backpack to the end of the rope. I found my gear buried under three feet of snow, and spent fifteen minutes carefully digging out the equipment. Once everything was set, I climbed, using mechanical ascenders that slide up on the rope but lock in when pulled taught. On my way up, I could hear the eerie sounds of neighboring crevasses creaking and groaning.

When I stuck my head out of the crevasse opening, I was greeted by two climbers who had descended the nearby West Rib Route. I was unaware that there were any other expeditions on the mountain besides the guided trip. The climbers, both Russian, helped me pull my equipment out of the crevasse. The three of us then tromped back to a well stocked ice cave that they had built weeks before. I spent the next three hours talking, eating, and drinking with my two new friends, both named Serge. The two of them showed me sacks of food left behind by expeditions long departed. The two Serges had come down to re-supply their expedition, and departed after filling their backpacks with food, leaving the ice cave and the left-over supplies to me.

Over the next five days, I regained my strength and sanity. I began my descent to the 9,600 foot airstrip on the afternoon of the fifth day. I only made it to just below Windy Corner, however, due to foul weather. Not let off easily by the mountain, the region clouded over as I took my last steps down Motorcycle Hill into the bowl at 11,000 feet the next day. By the time I reached Kahiltna Pass, the visibility had dropped to little more than twenty-five feet. The last of my descent into the emergency fly-out strip was harrowing, as winds gusted to over eighty miles per hour and visibility would vary from over one hundred yards to less than ten feet. By the time I staggered into camp, my backpack, sled, and hair were completely covered with rime ice, adding at least twenty pounds to my load. I found the small tent that contained a CB radio and started calling out to Talkeetna.

I wasn't able to make contact with anyone, as the batteries in the radio were nearly dead. There were two other parties waiting to fly out in addition to me, the guided trip and a group from Boston that had only made it to 9,600 feet. Neither was able to make radio contact. Conditions cleared the next day, and I was able to get a weak, broken connection with a lone miner in the bush. The connection lasted for only thirty seconds before our link cut out, but that was long enough for him to take down the necessary information. He relayed my message via radio telephone to a friend of his in Talkeetna who called the Park Service, who called Dave, who called Hudson Air Service. That afternoon, I was once again crammed into the hold of a Cessna 185 with a ton of equipment and other climbers. Taking off was exciting, but the flight was more a relief than an exhilaration, as I made it out just as another storm was moving into the area, and was beyond total exhaustion. Looking back at the gigantic massif, engulfed in a sea of clouds, I wondered if I would ever set foot in the region again. At that point in time, as I was speeding back to lower ground, my answer was a resounding no.

Photograph Page 88:
View from inside Crevasse; #171
This extremely rare perspective of a crevasse was made just seconds after I fell approximately eighty feet into this chasm. Snowbridges, which are weakened by the heat of the sun, hide these "slots", making travel on large glaciers extremely dangerous.

Photograph Page 92:
La Malinche and El Pico de Orizaba from summit ridge of Iztaccihuatl; #805
The volcanos of southern Mexico offer a high altitude experience without the dangers found on peaks such as Denali. Three of the seven highest mountains on the North American continent are found relatively close to Mexico City. Seen here is La Malinche, 14,636 feet (left), and El Pico de Orizaba, 18,885 feet (the third highest mountain in North America) from the summit ridge of Iztaccihuatl (17,338 feet).

Chapter Eight

Mexican Ice

⁸⁰⁵ *La Malinche and El Pico de Orizaba from Summit Ridge of Iztaccihuatl*

W ith my first Denali experience behind me, I left Talkeetna a little older, quite a bit thinner, and much wiser. For the remainder of my summer, I earned money at a fish cannery and then traveled throughout much of Alaska, including an excursion all the way to the Arctic Ocean. I took the "scenic" route back to California, exploring the states of Montana, Wyoming, Utah, and Colorado, where I stopped to see Mark and return his gear. As time progressed, my nightmares of Denali faded, replaced by dreams of exploring ever higher regions of the mountain. By the time I began my second year of university life, I was in the planning stages of my second attempt on the peak.

My goal for the year was to acquire the necessary gear, training, and fitness for a solo attempt on Denali—my decision to go alone reflected a desire to streamline the preparation process and took into account my short collaboration with Peter and Darren. I changed my academic direction from medicine to physical geography and geology, due in large part to what I had seen during the summer of 1990. I had also taken a Geology 1 class (on a whim) taught by a professor, Tracy Tingle, who would become a good friend in years to come. Changing my major made my sophomore year more enjoyable. I was able to learn about areas I had traveled to and understand some of the wild natural phenomena that I had witnessed. I continued to hone my photographic skills and sought critical advise from as many different sources as possible. I planned to make photography a significant part of my second attempt on Denali and garnered as much camera equipment as possible.

In order to acquire high altitude training, above that which is possible in the Sierra Nevada, I planned to climb the highest mountains in Mexico, El Pico de Orizaba (18,885 feet), Popocatapetl (17,882 feet), and Iztaccihuatl (17,338 feet), during my winter break. All three peaks are dormant volcanoes near Mexico City and are relatively non-technical to ascend. I bought a cheap airplane ticket for the early morning hours of the twenty-sixth of December, and prepared to take a minimal amount of climbing gear. During the months prior to my departure, I studied these peaks and surrounding regions thoroughly. Although I don't speak a word of Spanish, I decided to travel alone; I figured I wouldn't be around very many people while high in the mountains.

The first quarter of my sophomore year passed quickly. After a short Christmas break, I took off for south of the border. Upon arriving in Mexico City, I boarded a combi bus that took me to the small town of Amecameca, about forty miles southeast of the capitol. A taxi cab took me the remaining distance to the Tlamacas mountain hut at the foot of North America's fifth highest mountain, Popocatepetl. The giant, glacier capped volcano stands across a small valley from the continent's seventh highest mountain, Iztaccihuatl. The natural saddle that sits between the two is called Paso de Cortez, the point where Cortez rode through on his conquest of the region that is now Mexico City. I surveyed the area as much as possible, but soon retired to some secluded bushes as I had not slept in over twenty-four hours. My plan was to ascend Popocatepetl, Iztaccihuatl, and then travel west, to El Pico de Orizaba, the highest mountain in Mexico.

After acclimatizing at the Tlamacas hut, I made a number of excursions up the slopes of Popo, often returning due to headaches or nausea, both results of altitude sickness. Four days after arriving at the hut, I made a serious go for the summit. I left camp around two in the morning and traveled under the light of a near-full moon. By sunrise I had made it to over 15,000 feet and felt strong. A monotonous slog up volcanic ash and occasional patches of ice eventually brought me to the crater rim at 17,000 feet, where I nearly passed out due to a combination of thin air and choking sulfur fumes emanating from vents within the gigantic crater. To the west I could see the summit of the mountain, accessible from a long, dangerous traverse around the crater rim. I needed crampons to maneuver through the icy rocks along the top. The landscape was interesting: on one side of me was a steep glacier, on the other, a vertical wall which led to the bottom of the crater. One side fire, and the other side ice, and I was walking on the knife-edge that separates the two. By eleven o'clock in the morning, I reached the highest point. I didn't spend much time there, as the sulfur fumes were especially thick. Nonetheless, the view was magnificent. I could see the valley that encloses Mexico City (and all the smog), the beautiful sister volcano of Popo, Iztaccihuatl, and far in the distance, El Pico de Orizaba. Three hours after summiting, I was back at the hut, exhausted, blistered, and parched. I had climbed Popocatapetl, and now turned my sights toward Iztaccihuatl, but had no way to get to the base of the relatively untrammeled volcano, nearly fifteen miles distant. After resting, I sought a ride.

Although there are quite a number of climbers and tourists who come to the Tlamacas hut, few travel to Iztaccihuatl. The mountain is slightly lower and less accessible, but provides a wonderful wilderness outing. After searching for someone who was heading in that direction for a number of hours, I met a couple of climbers from Sweden. Not only were they going to Iztaccihuatl, but then on to Orizaba, and they were willing to give me a ride! The only problem was that they were leaving for Iztaccihuatl at one o'clock the next morning. I wanted to rest for a few days, but realized that I may not get another chance. I packed my belongings and settled in for as much sleep as I could possibly get.

After a meager re-charge that lasted only two hours, the three of us quickly packed and loaded our gear into their rented car. The two Swedes had intended to climb Iztaccihuatl together, but opted for ropeless travel, as it is a relatively non technical-climb similar to Popo. By two in the morning, the three of us were on our way, steadily ascending the lower slopes by moonlight. I wished that I could see the landscape. I imagined what it looked like, but knew that it would be quite different than what I pictured. By the time the sun was rising, I had made it to the crest of the three mile long summit ridge at 16,000 feet. I struggled up a crumbly, vertical cliff that was speckled with loose scree, tearing my hands as I gripped the rock and pulled myself up. I looked down to see the rock face disappear into darkness as I made my way onto the crest. Scanning eastward, I could see the silhouettes of Orizaba and a lower volcanic peak, Malinche. To the west, the full moon was just setting. I was at an amazing vantage point to witness an interesting phenomenon; just as the first rays of the sun's light diffracted over the eastern horizon, the last of the moon's disk dropped below the western horizon. I couldn't have asked for a clearer day, either. I quickly set up my camera to capture the event, and then relaxed thinking about how ideal my location was for witnessing a full moon set. A few minutes after the sun rose, winds picked up and cued me to move on. Although the ambient temperature at sixteen thousand feet during winter at night is well below freezing, constantly moving makes it possible to stay warm. Too long a rest, however, quickly reminds

765

Iztaccibuatl from Popocatepetl

Popocatepetl from Summit Ridge of Iztaccihuatl

826

97

one of the conditions, especially when the wind blows.

As I had been told, the summit ridge of Iztaccihuatl seemed to go on forever. I must have crested twenty false summits before arriving at the relatively undramatic mound of snow and ice that is the highest point. I checked my watch and noted that I had reached the summit of Iztaccihuatl twenty-three hours and fifty minutes after summiting Popo. I drank the last of my juice and began my descent. On my way, I felt weak and lethargic, a combination of exhaustion and altitude, and walked with a hunch in my back. I resisted the urge to stop and rest, however, as I knew I might fall asleep and end up stuck overnight without any camping gear. I passed one of the Swedes shortly after leaving the summit, as he was making his final march to the top. A brief conversation revealed that his partner had turned around further back. I decided to wait for him after he summited, so the two of us could go back together.

Our trek down the cliffs, snow slopes, and ice slopes was treacherous and grueling. At one point, I lost my footing and nearly fell down a five hundred foot precipice. The incident left me slightly shaken, but not too distraught, as I soon got back into my rhythm of descent. I watched cumulus clouds build around us as we traveled downward. I looked back toward the summit and noted that it was shrouded in darkness, soon to be deluged with hail, high winds and snow. Not wanting to get stuck in an afternoon storm, the two of us picked up speed. Although difficult to travel through, the terrain was spectacular. The colorful volcanic rock was covered in bright white glacial snow and ice. Ridges, cliffs, cornices, and icicles stood delicately juxtaposed in this high mountain realm. As with Denali, the scale was daunting.

By late afternoon the two of us made it down to easier ground. I was staggering and couldn't wait to get back to the car. My feet were a bloody mess, I was starving, and had been completely dehydrated (traveling at high altitudes requires a tremendous amount of fluid intake). Once back and relaxing at the Tlamacas hut, however, I felt great as my body's endorphins soothed the pain.

Popocatapetl, Iztaccihuatl, and El Pico de Orizaba are among a number of high volcanoes which mark the southern limit of the North American continent. The peaks formed as a result of the Caribbean plate subducting underneath the North American continental plate. This resulted in large upwellings of magma which eventually surfaced in dramatic, catastrophic events: volcanic eruptions. Unlike the smooth, low viscosity magma that creates spectacular rivers of molten rock in areas such as Hawaii and Iceland, the magma that created these mountains (and others such as the Cascades of the western United States) was very thick and highly viscous, due to its chemical composition containing a high proportion of the element Silicone. The result was a slow buildup pressure below the surface of the earth. Ultimately, this pressure was released in tremendous explosions which hurtled volcanic ash and superheated blocks of material many miles from the explosion site. Over the past 2.5 million years, many of these violent eruptions have occurred, producing the line of volcanoes that spans from Nevado de Colima on the western edge of Mexico, to El Pico de Orizaba and Cofre de Perote on the east coast. With each eruptive event, a layer of pyroclastic material (super heated rock and ash) was laid down at each location. From high on the slopes of Popocatepetl, I could see these different layers on large sections of exposed earth.

Although Popocatepetl, Iztaccihuatl, and El Pico de Orizaba all lie roughly along the nineteenth parallel where the climate is generally very warm, the peaks are high enough to promote glacial growth. It was interesting to compare and contrast Denali's glaciers with those of these three volcanoes. The glaciers throughout the Alaska Range are huge, and the landscape is dominated by them. The only slopes not covered by ice are those too steep for glaciers to develop. By comparison, the glaciers of the Mexican volcanoes are thin sheets of ice covering only the top few thousand feet of the peak. Where the surface of Alaska Range glaciers are usually soft snow, the volcanoes' glacial surfaces are very often hard ice. During the course of any given year, glaciers of the Alaska Range accumulate a tremendous amount of snow during the relatively warm, wet months of summer, and remain locked in brittle cold from autumn through spring. Although the temperatures of summertime days are high enough to melt much of the fallen snow (which then refreezes and eventually compacts the snow into ice, a process called sintering), the area is quickly re-frozen after the sun sets. During the months of fall through winter, the frigid climate never allows for any snowmelt, hence the expansive buildup of ice on Denali and other high mountains of the north country. The glaciers of the Mexican volcanoes, however, receive nourishing precipitation in the form of snow or hail almost every afternoon throughout the year, due to convective thunderstorms or weather fronts. This precipitation freezes during the night, as the high altitude air can hold very little heat once the sun sets. During the next day the intense tropical sun warms and melts the upper layers of glacial ice. The meltwater seeps into the lower levels of the glacier or runs off the side of the peaks, and is re-frozen during nighttime. This daily melt, replenishment, refreeze cycle is repeated throughout the year, creating glaciers which quickly react to the most minute changes in climate or weather. While perennial ice of far northern mountains moves through one cycle of growth per year, the glaciers of Popocatepetl, Iztaccihuatl, and El Pico de Orizaba have much shorter growth periods, sometimes as short as one day.

The two Swedes and I would take a day-long break before heading toward the town of Tlachichuca, at the base of El Pico de Orizaba. Although this Mexico trip was planned to train me for Denali, I was quickly becoming enthralled with the region and decided I would return to do more extensive travels in the area. It was as fascinating as any area I had yet been to, and many places, namely Iztaccihuatl, were sanctuaries of solitude. After packing my equipment, I viewed and photographed my last sunset from the Tlamacas hut. The next day the three of us were off, traveling through the countryside towards Orizaba.

The further we drove from Mexico City, the clearer the air, and the cleaner the countryside became. Fields of neatly groomed corn stood at the foot of many small volcanic peaks. Rolling topography meets steep cliffs and volcanic cones throughout this region. Once into Tlachichuca, the urban influence on the landscape is nearly imperceptible. We arrived just in time for the end of the Thursday street market. I bought some fruits and vegetables, and ate the most delicious tacos I had ever sunk my teeth into (and paid for them dearly a few weeks later). The three of us searched for a man named Senor Reyes, the person who owns the only vehicles capable of navigating the rough dirt roads to the hut at the base of the climb at an elevation just under 14,000 feet. In addition to owning the only "taxi" service, Senor Reyes also owns the only telephone, grocery store, and gas station, as well as the only place to spend the night. It was not difficult to find Senior Reyes.

The evening spent in Tlachichuca was great. The Gulf of Mexico lies just seventy-five miles from Tlachichuca, and the evening brought wonderfully cool breezes. A few hours after the sun set, the nighttime sky became filled with stars. I could make out the Milky Way and a number of hard to see constellations. It was one of the clearest nights I had ever seen. The three of us retired to some bunks inside Senor Reyes' "fortress" (he had quite a house, completely enclosed by a twenty foot wall), and rested well.

The next day, the three of us packed our belongings into the back of an old flatbed truck with some rickety railings along the sides and rear of the bed. I was amazed that this mufflerless monstrosity could pull out of Senor Reyes' home, much less make it to nearly 14,000 feet. While we secured our belongings, the driver, a rough and dirty guy with two teeth and a soiled hat, checked everything out and finished off a bottle of tequila. I opted to stay in the back while the two Swedes crammed into the cab. The view would be amazing and I wanted to be in a good spot to bail out if necessary. We pulled onto a cobblestone road that leads out of town, just as the sky was beginning to turn gray with billowy clouds. As the truck slowly ascended the lower hills at the foot of Orizaba, the condition of the road grew wretched. I increasingly relied on the wobbly wooden railings for support.

For the next one and a half hours, I held on for the most exciting vehicular adventure of my life (probably the most objectively hazardous part of the entire climb). I couldn't believe that we were traveling on any kind of established road. It looked like our driver just aimed the vehicle up the side of the hill and stepped on the gas pedal. We passed through small settlements and mountainous agricultural fields, then went into a forested zone. The higher we got, the colder and cloudier the conditions became. Near the end of the drive, we were in mist. I was wearing only a T-shirt, and was shivering, but would have to wait until the ride was over before I could get to warmer clothes. By late in the afternoon, we broke out of the forested area and traveled the remaining miles to the stone Piedre Grande hut. A large group of Americans were waiting for their ride down, and we quickly swapped places while they told me about the route above. After stashing my gear in the large structure,

I watched the taxi jostle into the forest and out of sight. Directly above the hut was the Glaciar de Jamapa, where the Ruta Norte (Northern Route) ascends to the summit. The hut is on the far northern aspect of the mountain and looks out over the eastern coast of Mexico. As the sun set, a large "V" shaped shadow was cast atop the soft pink blanket of clouds which hid the Gulf Coast from view (this shadow was the actual shadow of the volcano). I always enjoy standing above a layer of clouds.

Although I had been well acclimatized on Popocatepetl and Iztaccihuatl, I felt a slight headache coming on after a few hours at Piedre Grande. In addition to the two Swedes and myself, there was a large group of Germans and some Mexican climbers. The hut at Piedre Grande can sleep over sixty people, and it was packed full. In addition to their climbing gear, the German team brought along eight cases of beer. A few hours after I laid down to go to sleep, most of it was gone and the group was singing Bavarian beer hall songs. It didn't bother me too much, but one of the Swedes finally had it, and told them to shut up. They didn't listen, however, and kept on singing. Around 1:00 a.m., the three of us packed our gear and started up toward the summit, just as the last of the Germans was passing out.

The route up Orizaba is straight forward. A well marked trail leads out of Piedre Grande to where the glacier begins at 16,000 feet. At first I used my head-lamp for navigation, but once out of the gully where the ascent begins, the near full moon shed plenty of light on the landscape. I maintained a slow, steady pace to the base of the glacier, where I put on my crampons. There was still no hint of sunrise, and I figured I was making good time. Once again I was separated from the two Swedes, one turned around shortly after starting out, and the other was a few hundred yards ahead of me. The climb up the glacier was spectacular. Illuminated by the moon's light and nothing else, I climbed upward. The only sounds were of the steel spikes of my crampons squeakily penetrating the hardened, Styrofoam-like snow. An hour after starting up the glacier, I noticed a bright flash from below. I looked out to see the lights of the town of Veracruz, 16,000 feet below me and seventy-five miles away, and wondered what was going on. The altitude hampered my ability to think or reason. At first I wondered if a bomb exploded, but then I saw the flash again—it was a lightning storm. I knelt on the snow and rested against my ice ax to watch a number of thunderclouds over the Gulf of Mexico light up with bursts of electrical discharge. Although over a mile below me, I was mesmerized. I had never looked down on a thunderstorm before.

The glacier became progressively steeper as I made my way up. I was glad that it was nighttime, as I didn't want to see where or how far I would go if I fell. I met up with the Swede just as the first light of the rising sun illuminated the eastern sky. According to his altimeter, we were at 17,500 feet, and the slope was quite steep. I went to shoot a photograph of my friend climbing away from me and realized that my camera was out of film. I shed my gloves to fiddle with the camera just as the wind picked up. My fingers instantly went numb and the situation was complicated by having to touch the metal of the camera with unprotected skin. Delicately, I pulled the film canister from the camera back and stuck it in my jacket pocket, and while balancing on the exposed, icy slope, I loaded a roll of fresh film. The job was tedious, my hands felt nothing and were clumsy, but eventually I got everything squared away. After warming my hands inside my gloves, I continued onward.

As I climbed, I looked out over the awesome Gulf of Mexico. The thunderclouds which brilliantly lit up the night sky were broken apart by the time the sun rose above the horizon. By 7:30 in the morning, I reached the crater rim and flopped down on the snow for a rest. A small group of climbers who had just reached the summit passed me on their way down. My Swedish friend was with them, and he congratulated me on reaching the crater rim. The summit was not far off. After taking a few pictures and wishing the group luck on their descent, I took the last steps toward the top of the mountain. At 8:00 a.m., I was on the highest point in Mexico. I shared the small patch of snow with one of the Germans. Neither of us spoke each other's language, nor Spanish, but we shared some food and drink, and took summit photographs for one another. I took some pictures of the near full moon setting over Popocatepetl and Iztaccihuatl in the west, and the cloud shrouded Gulf of Mexico to the east. The wind was gusting hard, and I decided to get down as soon as possible. I bade farewell to my new friend, who was waiting for some of his partners to reach the summit, and headed down.

The descent was uneventful. After making it through the most dangerous section, I breathed a sigh of relief and picked up speed. Once down to 16,000 feet, I took off my crampons and jogged back to Piedre Grande. Upon arrival, the two Swedish guys congratulated me and we all relaxed with some beer, compliments of the Germans. I had completed the "Mexican Trilogy", climbing the three highest mountains of that country, and felt ready for Denali (at least the altitude part of it, anyway).

I am often asked which of the three was my favorite. After asking myself this same question over and over, I came to the conclusion that none were my actual "favorite". On Popo, I laughed and socialized the most. Iztaccihuatl provided the best wilderness experience, and El Pico de Orizaba granted me some of the most spectacular views and best beer I ever had. I spent the next week traveling about central and southern Mexico and then returned to California, where I continued school and began the final preparations for my second Denali expedition.

Photograph Page 96:
Iztaccihuatl from Popocatepetl; #765
Iztaccihuatl, North America's seventh highest mountain, is a seldom traveled peak that lies due north of the slightly higher Popocatepetl. The high volcanoes of Mexico provide excellent grounds for high altitude training, and are often climbed as preparations for Denali attempts. The long summit ridge of Iztaccihuatl can be seen in this image.

Photograph Page 97:
Popocatepetl from Summit Ridge of Iztaccihuatl; #826
The views from the summit ridge of Iztaccihuatl are spectacular. The long, intricate ridge has many discouraging "false summits", and makes for an exhausting climb. To the south, the snow-capped, cone-shaped Popocatepetl can be seen from high on this ridge.

14891   *Saint Elias Mountains from the Air*

Photograph This Page:

Saint Elias Mountains from the Air; #14891
The ten highest mountains in the North American continent lie in three major ranges; the Alaska Range, the Mexican volcanoes, and the Saint Elias Mountains. The Saint Elias Mountains lie to the southeast of Denali along the Alaska-Yukon border, and are even less accessible than the Alaska Range. The continent's second highest mountain is found here, Mount Logan, at 19,850 feet above sea level.

Photograph Page 106:

Preparing to Leave Base Camp; #1859
Due to my previous year's mishap at 14,200 feet, I constructed a special self extrication system that was designed to bridge any crevasses that I could possibly fall into. The day I began my 1991 climb arrived clear and calm. The conditions were so good that Denali could be seen in its entirety (set back behind foreground peaks and ridges).

Chapter Nine

Return to Alaska

Preparing to Leave Base Camp

U pon returning to California, I settled in once again to the rigors of academia. Although still months away, I also devoted as much time and effort towards planning my June departure for Alaska. Unlike the previous year, I knew exactly what I needed and exactly how to go about garnering the necessary gear. One of my biggest problems was designing a system to protect me from falling to my death, in the event of breaking through a snowbridge. I brainstormed many ideas, but the one which I finally pursued was a system involving a ten foot long aluminum ladder. I went to the local hardware store and purchased one that fit the bill. I cut out the middle rung, and attached high-strength climbing webbing on both sides of the rig, in order to suspend it from my backpack. The system worked with me standing "inside" the ladder (where the middle rung had been cut out), attaching the tail end of the ladder to the sled, and having my backpack's waist harness suspend the entire system. I clipped my climbing harness into the rung directly in front of where I stood; in the event that I broke through a snowbridge, the five feet of ladder sticking in front of me and the five in back would either bridge the crevasse or distribute my weight over a much wider area, allowing me to climb free and out of danger, hopefully.

By mid-May, I had acquired almost all the equipment necessary. My ladder was ready (complete with a fluorescent paint job). I had a good supply of food, my car was in travel shape, and I had suitable clothing (no cotton this time). I called Dave Lee of Talkeetna Air Taxi and had him stash away any left over food from previous expeditions. Dave would also let me exchange work for my flight onto the glacier. I would chop wood for him and do other odd chores. I traded in my old camera and lenses for a new Nikon Fm2 (a fully manual and very rugged camera body) and three lenses, a 28mm, 50mm, and a 70-210mm zoom lens. I also purchased one hundred rolls of film at wholesale, from a volume discount center. I carried a plentiful supply of batteries and lens cleaner, as well as polarizing and skylight filters. One of my most important acquisitions, however, was a large, heavy duty tripod. I was told that it would be crazy to lug that big piece of equipment up so high, but it was worth it to me. In addition to the tripod, I bought a quarter-twenty threaded bolt (the standard thread size for tripod mounts) and hacked off the bolt head. I took the remaining headless bolt and melted it into the handle of one of my ski poles and attached a retaining nut on it. I also attached a similar device onto the head of my ice ax. My plan was to take the tripod as high as 17,200 feet, then use the ski pole or ice ax for a camera stabilizer on the high slopes.

Although I had been preparing for the second Denali trip for a full six months, I was racing to make sure everything was in order right up to the night before departure. My route to Talkeetna would be identical to the previous year, beginning on Interstate 5 and eventually ending up on the Alaska Highway. Unlike the year before, however, I took a night to rest after my last final exam before departing. My Volkswagen was packed to the hilt. Inside was enough food and supplies to last for weeks, enough film and camera equipment for months, and on the roof was a large fluorescent ladder. At 9:00 a.m. on June 7, 1991, I was Alaska bound once again.

The first part of the trip was the loneliest. It's never easy leaving the safety of friends, especially to go on a trip where so many things can go wrong. More than once, I nearly pulled over and turned around, starting is always the hardest part.

It wasn't long, however, before my solemn attitude wore off. I breezed through California, Oregon, and all the way to the border of Canada in one sweep. By the time I arrived, the Canadian border was closed, so I bedded down on the side of the road by a gas station. Unlike the year before, when my whole trip was shrouded in mystery and anxiety of the unknown, I knew what lay ahead. I had a clear and defined plan of action and would not stray off course. The morning arrived quickly. I packed up and was the first person through the gate that day. With everything in proper order and all necessary funds, I was in and out of the crossing station in less than ten minutes. During my first hours in Canada, I began speculating on the excitement that lay ahead—What would the mountain be like this year? Would my car completely break down somewhere, hundreds of miles from any major town? Would I go flat broke with no job and have to sell everything just to make it home? Would I allow my fears to get the best of me and return to California? Or would I never return home again? So much lay ahead, this was not to be the last of my speculative and hopeful states of mind.

I passed familiar landmarks throughout the day; towns, mountains, even road signs. I drove by Hell's Gate on the Frazier River and fell into a trance as I traveled up the arid Frazier Valley. Just like the previous year, I aimed to get to Alaska as soon as possible. Although I wanted to make extended trips in regions I passed en route, I had a schedule to keep. I made many mental notes for future excursions, however, and viewed landscape with a high degree of appreciation and understanding due to my education. As the day wore on, I traveled through the logging town of Prince George and then headed through relatively uninhabited wooded land, with my eye on the distant Canadian Rockies. Once north of Prince George, the Caribou Highway 97 becomes significantly less crowded. I enjoyed hogging the entire road, driving down the middle divider and looking out at the landscape. I finally ran out of gas in a town called Hudson's Hope, where I was forced to spend the night as no gas station was open.

My route followed a course away from the Rockies and into less dramatic, rolling topography. I was on the Alaska Highway once more, and although I would pass through the Rocky Mountains again, the stretch of road from where I joined the highway until just beyond the town of Fort Nelson is relatively featureless. By late evening, however, I climbed into the heights of the Rocky Mountains. I didn't remember much of this from the previous year, mostly due to the late hour I traveled through it then, but the scenery was incredible and I was glad to be able to view it during well lit hours. Just as the day began to give way to nightfall, I crossed the 60th parallel and was in the Yukon. After fueling my car in the town of Watson Lake, I checked out the "sign wall", a large wall with signs of towns from all around the world nailed onto it. There was a "Visalia" sign, my old home town. I was baffled by the irony of a piece of stolen public property from my home town ending up on a wall next to the side of the Alaska Highway in the Yukon. That evening, I continued until I could no longer keep my eyes open. I pulled over just outside of the Yukon's capitol, Whitehorse, and pitched camp in a gravel quarry.

I was only about twenty hours away from Talkeetna. I slept as long as I could before beginning the last leg of the drive. After checking my car's mechanical situation and eating breakfast, I drove off. My anxiety built as I traveled past Kluane and into Alaska. I lost track of time, and like the previous year, was amazed to see a rainbow at midnight. Near the town of Glenallen, my vehicle began having trouble. I refueled one last time, never shutting the car off out of fear that it would not start again. In addition to the engine problem, my left rear tire went flat after rolling through a dirt section of highway. Because I was so anxious to get to Talkeetna, I used a can of flat-fixer to seal the hole and inflate the tube instead of replacing the tire. I was, however, only five hours from my destination. My car had made it this far and I was determined to get it and its cargo all the way, even if it meant pushing.

For the next few hours, I fought fatigue by sticking my head out the moving car to check the wheel, and watched my odometer rack up miles. Finally, I breathed a sigh of relief as I turned onto the road marked by the "Talkeetna 15" sign. My car's condition, however, was rapidly deteriorating. I figured that the gas pump was going out as the car ran rough and often sputtered, but only intermittently. After cresting a small hill, I could see the magnificent Alaska Range, bathed in the crimson light of the early morning Alaskan sun. I pulled off to the side of the road at the Mount McKinley overlook and photographed the region. I was standing above the Susitna River, only a few hundred feet above sea level, and could make out all the levels of the Alaska Range, from the low foothills, to the very summit of Denali itself. The sky was completely clear except for some clouds which hovered above the peaks and provided a dramatic backdrop to the peaks. The air was still and there was dead silence. After taking many images of the area, I returned to my car to drive the remaining half mile to Talkeetna Air Taxi. Upon turning the ignition key however, I realized that I should have never turned the car off. The motor turned over, but did not start. Too tired to fiddle with the engine, I secured everything in the car, rolled it down the small hill, and pushed it all the way to the airport. I had finally made it.

I was so exhausted, I barely had my sleeping bag rolled out on the ground behind Dave Lee's office before I fell asleep. I laid unconscious for a good eight hours before I awoke to the roar of Dave's Cessna. The day was great, hardly a cloud in the sky and the temperature was warm. I did my morning rituals and then went inside the office, just as one of TAT's aircraft was rolling out the runway. I was surprised to see Dave behind the desk, but nevertheless happy, as he was a familiar face.

"Hello, Ed!" Dave always seemed to be in a good mood.

"It's good to be here. Who's flying your plane?"

"Oh, that's a guy we've got working for us for the season, it's been so busy that I needed to hire another pilot this year."

It was good to see Dave, and it wasn't long before he had to run out to fly a group of sightseers around the range.

"Sorry I can't talk much now, Ed. I've gotta run, but tell me about your trip when I get back."

Once I was completely awake, I wasted no time getting my flight scheduled and my climb registered with the rangers. I would fly into base camp the next day, the twelfth. Although they discouraged traveling solo, the rangers were happy that I had devised a self protection system for glacier travel. I listened to what they had to say about the dangers of mountaineering on Denali for the second time and watched the video. Once I took care of my pre-climb formalities, I returned to my car and prepared my gear. Linda showed me the food that was left over from previous expeditions and I added some of it to my collection. I carefully loaded my large bag which would be strapped in a sled, and then filled my backpack and rigged my crevasse ladder. With everything ready to go, I neatly piled my belongings inside the rear of Dave's office and went into town to eat and take pictures.

Throughout the day, the weather remained picturesque. I kept my fingers crossed that the conditions would prevail through the next day, and hopefully throughout the next few weeks. I met a few climbers who had been in the range and found out that the season had been less than ideal thus far. It had only been in the last few days that the weather cleared. I optimistically reasoned that since there had been such a bad spell of weather for so long, the next few weeks would be good ones. I would just have to acclimatize well and stay away from crevasses. By evening, I was back at Talkeetna Air Taxi, making sure that I had everything in order for my big climb. After talking with Dave for a while and catching up on the mountain's news, I slipped into my sleeping bag and waited anxiously for the next day to arrive, trying in vain to get some rest.

Chapter Ten

Into The Big Alaskan Sky

2091 *Clouds above McKinley River at Sunset*

I awoke on the twelfth of June to bright sunshine. The sun had just popped into the window, and warm beams of light struck my face and sleeping bag. I immediately hopped into my mountaineering clothes, including my heavy, double plastic boots, then went and got fifty rolls of film from my car, thirty of Kodachrome 64, and twenty of Kodachrome 25. I stuffed the film and other camera necessities into a large waist pack that would be with me throughout the trip. I bade my car farewell, shut the door, and walked out onto the tarmac where Dave was preparing his plane.

"Glad to see you could join us."

Dave was checking the fuel on his aircraft and seemed to be ready to fly.

"Are we all right to go today?"

"Yeup, looks like the weather is going to hold."

In addition to myself, there were two "flight-seers" who were going to be flying with us. Dave either flies around Denali, or lands and lets the tourists throw snowballs on a genuine Alaskan glacier.

I pulled all my gear over to the plane and Dave carefully loaded it into the fuselage of the Cessna. The ladder barely fit into the aircraft, and all my other gear was placed around it. The two sight-seers climbed in the rear of the craft, helped secure the gear, and then buckled themselves into their seats. I looked around the tarmac and stamped my feet on the last terra firma I would stand on for weeks before climbing aboard the plane. Once inside, I looked around to gauge how I would shoot photographs from the moving craft.

Cessnas are wonderful airplanes for photography. They have a high wing and only one strut, allowing a relatively wide angle lens to be used without worrying about an obtrusive black line showing up on the final image. The Cessna 185 has a feature that allows the small slat windows to be flipped up for unobstructed photographs. I would like to have taken the door off in order to have a truly free view of the landscape below, but that would mean 120 to 150 mile per hour winds roaring by my face and increased piloting difficulties for Dave. On my camera, I had a 50mm lens with a polarizer. The filter would cut out any annoying reflections on the glass I was shooting through, should I choose not to flip the window up. I had eight rolls of film at the ready, sitting on top of other gear in my half opened waist pack tucked between my feet. I would end up shooting all eight rolls during the forty-five minute flight. Because the plane would be moving rather quickly and vibrating wildly, I preset the shudder speed to 1/500 of a second to ensure sharp images.

After the passengers and gear were in the plane, Dave locked everything down and made sure we had our seat belts on. After adjusting some controls and checking the aircraft's diagnostic gauges, Dave logged his flight plan and kicked over the engine. I felt a surge of adrenaline move through me as we began to roll out to take off position. I watched the huge letters which spelled out "TALKEETNA" go by as we moved. After taxying into position, Dave rolled down the aircraft's flaps, checked the surface controls one last time, then throttled the engine and we tore off into the huge Alaskan sky. Rising above the trees, I could see the massive cumulus clouds built up along the front of the Alaska Range, partially hiding Denali and the other huge peaks of the region. Dave banked the plane and we made a 120° turn. Denali was now dead ahead. I worked my camera furiously, beginning with photographs of the confluence of the Susitna, Traleika, and Cook rivers (Talkeetna is an Athabaskan word meaning "the joining of three rivers"). As the craft steadily gained altitude, we rose above some of the lower clouds hanging over the tundra, and some of the highest peaks started popping into view. The sense of speed in a plane is lost as it climbs away from stationary reference points. Suddenly, from behind one of the clouds, an airplane from another air taxi service whizzed by on its way back to Talkeetna—a close look revealed that it was one of Doug Geeting's planes, possibly the one I flew in last year. Even though it was a good half mile away, the two of us passed each other at such an incredible speed it was frightening.

Dave was giving his usual "tour guide" talk to the other two passengers, sitting wide eyed in the back seats. I was oblivious to everything but capturing the amazing scenes on film. With my focusing ring locked on the infinity mark, I shot in all directions and varied my compositions, putting every ounce of energy and concentration into getting great images. Dave continued to identify the sights and fly the plane, all while turning around to talk to the other passengers. This made the two guys a little nervous (Dave laughingly told me about this afterward). He's flown this route so many times, however,

Tundra and Rivers below Clouds

1661

that he can do it with his eyes closed. We flew away from the lowlands of the Susitna River Valley and over the mineral rich Peters and Dutch hills. It is here that the largest of the Alaska Range glaciers terminate in large jumbles of boulders, ice, and rock. Shortly after flying above the foothills of the range, we entered a world of bare rock and ice. The large, puffy cumulus clouds were behind us, our sights set on the massifs of Denali, Mount Foraker, and Mount Hunter. We were flying up the thirty-nine mile long Kahiltna glacier, a huge "river" of ice, advancing only five to ten yards per year (a fairly average rate for such a glacier). Along the flanks of the main stream of ice were countless smaller tributary glaciers merging with the main Kahiltna. These smaller glaciers are fed by even smaller cirque glaciers (the smallest type of glacier, with the erosion pattern of a large bowl). The view from above was magnificent. I couldn't have asked for better weather. The entire glacial system, the sheer rock and ice walls, the knife edged ridges, the intricate snow formations, and Denali itself, made for a spectacular setting. Nearly a year before, I swore I would never return. Now that I was seeing this area again, however, I couldn't believe I had ever wished to not come back.

I would be living in this realm for the better part of a month, if not more, on top of 3,000+ foot thick sheets of ice, under avalanche prone slopes, on top of knife-edged ridges. Although I had spent a significant amount of time in this region the year before, there was no way I could prepare myself for what I was now seeing. We flew within fifty feet of a huge vertical granite wall, capped by a hanging glacier. I wondered how often it dropped huge chunks of ice onto the landscape below. The environment was undeniably one of the most impressive and humbling places I have ever been to.

Dave flew us past the west ridge of Mount Hunter and the southeast fork of the Kahiltna Glacier. We flew further up the glacier to take a closer look at Denali, particularly the West Buttress, where I would be climbing. Dave banked the plane to go back to base camp and land, and I shot about ten photographs of the best view of the mountain I had yet seen. I photographed the entire West Buttress, the high slopes of the peak, and a graceful summit lenticular cloud, all with the backdrop of a nearly black sky. As we approached base camp, I could see some tents and tracks in the snow made by climbers on their way to Denali. We flew low over a field of crevasses, some of which were so large they could swallow an entire rope team. The plane banked away from the crevasse field and up into the valley of the Southeast Fork. Dave looked more serious than he had during the rest of the flight. He dropped the flaps and the plane slowed to landing speed. I put my camera safely in my lap and watched as the snowy surface occupied an increasingly greater area of my field of view. I looked up just as the aircraft smoothly touched down on its two front skis. Soon after initial contact, the rear tail skid made contact. Dave gunned the engine to get us to the unloading zone, boosted the tail of the craft around, and shut off the engine. I was once again at Kahiltna Base.

Dave and I unloaded my gear while the two other passengers romped on the glacier. I pulled out my backpack and then wrestled the large "mule bag", packed with ninety pounds of gear, out of the craft and onto a sled. I would tow this sled up to my previous year's high point at the ice bowl (14,200 feet), where further travel with it would be impractical. Once I got everything hauled over to where I was going to pitch camp for the night, Dave bid me farewell and wished me luck. He then prepared to fly back to Talkeetna, and got the two sightseers secured in the plane. With his passengers safely buckled in, Dave started the Cessna and skidded down the glacier. Shortly thereafter the craft popped into the air, and soon became just a speck against the awesome southeast ridge of Mount Foraker. I watched until the blue plane disappeared behind a ridge to the south of base camp, then began to dig my campsite.

Photograph Page 112:
Clouds above McKinley River at Sunset;
#2091
An incredible sweep of lake-speckled tundra lies to the north of Denali. This wild landscape becomes lit up brilliantly as the low Alaskan sun rises or sets. While camped at 11,500 feet on Denali, I photographed this ethereal scene as a storm was breaking up, juxtaposing bits of quickly moving clouds on the broad landscape during a midnight sunset.

Photograph Page 115:
Tundra and Rivers below Clouds; #1661
The relatively flat region to the south of Denali and the Alaska Range is dominated by rivers and lakes. The rivers found here originate at the termini of the many large glaciers of the region. While flying onto the mountain for my 1991 attempt, I had an incredible view of the landscape through the cottonball-like cumulus clouds.

Chapter Eleven

Racing up the Kahiltna

1930   *Camp at the 9,600 Foot Level of the Kahiltna Glacier*

It didn't take me long to set up camp at Kahiltna Base, a surprise since I was so out of practice. After preparing my shelter, I walked over to the radio hut to see who was operating base camp for the season. One person, a woman named Annie, had come up the year before on a flight seeing tour and decided to return to run everything. She had been on the mountain for a month already and would remain for three more weeks. The other operator, Pam, had just flown up one week earlier. I couldn't believe that Annie had been in base camp for an entire month and planned to stay for the better part of another. I sat down with the two base camp managers and some others at camp, and discussed the condition of the mountain for most of the remainder of the day.

There were a couple of climbers who were guides for Rainier Mountaineering, an assistant guide named Alex, and an apprentice, Ned. They had returned from the 9,600 foot level with a sick client and were going to go back up as soon as the sun set and the region cooled off (freezing the snowbridges solid). Alex was a professional mountain guide, spending upwards of three months on Denali each climbing season and guiding throughout the globe during the remainder of the year. Ned was a professional skier and student in Washington State. This was his first trip to Denali and his first guiding experience. Both were well acclimatized and knew the condition of the lower Kahiltna intimately, as they had been up and down it many times over the last few days. I tried to get as much information about the state of the glacier from them as I could, but there was only so much they could tell me, and none of it could fully prepare me for an unknown situation.

The day flew by. It didn't seem like much time had passed before I watched the sun set behind Mount Crosson, and Alex and Ned made their way onto the main Kahiltna. The few others at camp waddled and hustled into their tents with nightfall. I stayed outside, however, for a few more hours with my camera to get some sunset shots of the surrounding area. It was my first night on the glacier and I was eager to capture some of the patterns and formations around me on film. The temperature dropped dramatically while I made images of the Kahiltna region, and it was not long before I retired myself. As I restlessly tossed and turned in my sleeping bag, I couldn't help but speculate about the following day's events. I was very excited about departing and soon worried that my excitement would prevent me from getting any sleep. It wasn't until around 3:00 a.m. that I passed out.

I woke on the morning of June thirteenth in a very groggy and disoriented state. A dense layer of frost clung to the inside wall of my tent, indicating that temperatures fell well below freezing during the night. I checked my camera for condensation and then curled back into my warm bag. It was 7:30 a.m. and the sun had not yet risen over Mount Hunter. A half hour later, I noticed a small glimmer of sunlight on the wall of my tent, the warm rays were my cue to jump out of sleep and motivate. I packed my sleeping bag and tent, cooked breakfast, and got dressed. The National Park Service was flying training missions in their newly acquired helicopter, an Aerospatial

Photograph This Page:
Snowshoeing up Main Kahiltna Glacier; #1881
In order to protect myself from potential crevasse falls, I devised a system that would hold me up should I break through a weakened snowbridge. The strange system was incredibly difficult to travel with, as it was awkward and added over twenty pounds to my load.

Llama, a high altitude machine which is capable of hovering over the summit of Denali with a five hundred pound payload. Just as I was finishing loading my gear into my backpack and sled, I could hear the CLAP—CLAP of the approaching helicopter. The craft moved gracefully through the thin air and made a perfect landing on the east side of the glacial runway and then shut down. I watched as a couple of rangers jumped out and walked over to the base camp hut. I continued to go about my preparations and figured that I would be able to set out within fifteen minutes. Everything was falling into shape quickly, and I had only a few remaining pieces of equipment that needed to be tied down.

After double and triple checking lash points, knots, potential weak links, and mentally checking off all my gear, I began harnessing myself in. While I put on my backpack and sled, one of the park rangers came over to warn me one last time.

"Are you sure you want to go through with this?"

"Well, I don't think that I'm going to change my mind now."

"Just stay safe, and don't do anything foolish."

I thanked him for his concern and then finished my preparations. Once all my gear was securely connected and harnessed, I put on my snowshoes and started out.

"Good-bye, hope to see you soon."

I couldn't think of anything more creative. My goal for the day was to make it to the base of Ski Hill, near where the northeast fork and the main fork of the Kahiltna Glacier merge. The weather was as good as it could be. I was thankful for this, and hoped that it would hold out. The short downhill stretch out of base camp provided me with the first practical test of how well my ladder system would work. During the previous year's expedition, I was constantly dumbfounded by my heavy sled flipping over and sliding past me on this stretch. Because my sled this year was being pulled by the end of my rigid ladder, it remained where it was supposed to be, always five feet directly behind me.

I quickly descended to the main Kahiltna. I set up my camera and took some self timer photographs of my system in action and then skirted the foot of Mount Francis on my way up the gigantic lobe of ice. I cold see Ski Hill far ahead, but couldn't catch a glimpse of where I would camp, as I was in the middle of a tremendous crevasse field (the one I saw from the airplane) and was constantly weaving in and out and up and down snow bridges and glacial undulations. I knew that every time I put my foot down, I might careen through a weakened snowbridge. Ever thoughtful of last year's experience, I put all urges for rest, food, or fluids behind me, aimed for Ski Hill, and went like mad. Of course, when carrying a total of over 120 pounds in pack and sled, going like mad is little more than brisk walking. Nevertheless, I pushed onward with all my strength. Since I was beginning my climb late in the season, when temperatures can surpass ninety-five degrees Fahrenheit in direct sunlight near the surface of the Kahiltna, I wanted to reach my destination before the region warmed enough to significantly weaken what snow bridges I would be crossing.

At ten o'clock in the morning, I had made it to the confluence of the east fork and main fork of the Kahiltna, half way to my destination. Ahead was a section of bumps and hills, a sign of a fractured glacier, but nothing too bad. I rested for a few minutes at a spot that seemed to be safe, and took some pictures. Although the suspension system for my ladder rig was working well, it was taking its toll on my waist in the form of blisters. My backpack, heavily laden with gear and food, was making my body sore as well. I didn't rest for too long, as the more I waited, the more comfortable I would become and consequently more reluctant to carry on. I picked up and kept going. It wasn't long before I had made it to the opening of the northeast fork, near where I planned to camp. I peered up the valley, called by some "the valley of death", due to the extreme danger of burial by avalanche ever present in this narrow and steep-sided glacial trough. Climbers approaching the Cassin Ridge, West Rib, or any of the South Face routes must travel up the Northeast Fork to arrive at their destinations. The approach up this valley is one of the most objectively hazardous aspects of any climb on the South Face.

By 11:30 in the morning, I could see my destination, only a few hundred yards away. It was a level section of the glacier where there was a low probability of hidden crevasses. There were signs that others had recently stayed there, but I hadn't come across anyone since leaving Kahiltna Base. The final steps into camp were grueling, I was tired, hungry, and the sun beat down with a vengeance. I was happy to unclip from my ladder and other gear and give my body a rest. Just as I sat down to relax, however, I heard and felt a tremendous rumble. I looked around frantically and spotted a massive avalanche roaring down the vertical northeast face of Kahiltna Dome, about one and a half miles away. I pulled out my camera and managed to get two photographs of the plume of ice and snow crashing down onto the surface of the Glacier. Although I was well out of the avalanche's range, I shuddered as I watched the tons of debris race down 3,500 vertical feet in a matter of

West Ridge of Mount Hunter

1826

seconds. It was a blunt reminder of the region's dangers.

After pitching camp, I spent the remainder of the day avoiding direct sunlight, eating and drinking, and trying to decide what camera compositions I would use for the various scenes around me. Late in the day, as the low light cast long shadows on the landscape, I emerged from my shelter and set up my camera on its tripod. I watched as clouds materialized around some of the high peaks in the region. I was pleased to have some atmospheric diversity after the long day of unhindered sunlight, but knew that these nascent clouds probably meant an oncoming storm. Since I was not carrying a radio, I could not find out what the weather forecast was for the region, but knew that most forecasts for the Alaska Range were rarely correct, anyway.

As the day passed, the conditions around my camp turned calm. Being alone in such a serene but wild region gave me a feeling of tremendous isolation. During the day, I carefully examined the features of the landscape surrounding my camp. Because one of my primary goals of the trip was to photographically record what I saw on the expedition, I concentrated deeply on what I was witnessing around me at the time. I watched the low Alaskan summer sun peer in and out of ephemeral cloud formations and shed light on the different geologic and glacial formations. The infinitely varying scenes both dumbfounded and inspired me to try and capture what I was witnessing on film.

After many hours, I crawled inside my tent and fell asleep. It was considerably easier to get rest the second night than the first, as I was physically exhausted. I don't remember dreaming anything, and I awoke to conditions signaling an oncoming storm. After quickly dressing and packing, I photographed myself with my ladder, "rigged up", and began the ascent of Ski Hill.

Ski Hill is the first significant topographical relief on the West Buttress, and although not very steep in comparison to the rest of the mountain, was still exhausting, given the large amount of cargo I was carrying between my backpack and sled. I powered up the first quarter of the grade, but was forced to drop to my knees in pulmonary agony at the first level portion of the hill. I rested for about five minutes and then sucked in my gut in mental and physical preparation and lurched onward, trying to forget about the extreme danger of hidden crevasses in the region. Throughout the day, I watched the area become increasingly stormy—the morning began with moderate winds and high cirrus clouds. By mid-morning, there were lenticulars draping the summits of the highest peaks of the region, a sure sign of an oncoming storm. By late afternoon, I could see my day's destination, the 9,600 foot level on the glacier where I "evacuated" from roughly one year before. By the time I reached my goal, I was barely able to dig a snow wall and erect my small tent before visibility approached zero and winds accelerated to over fifty miles per hour. Although the weather was turning sour, I felt assured, as I was dug in deeply and had ample food to wait out any degree of inclement weather.

Once I had set up camp and eaten my dinner, I relaxed and watched the amorphous cloud formations continuously change shape. My dinner, as the previous night's, consisted of spicy top ramen and sugar coated oatmeal, very appetizing at that point. It wasn't long before I was out with my camera, recording what I could on film. I watched in amazement as the swiftly moving clouds socked the region in and then "opened up", exposing the entire Kahiltna region, which appeared more beautiful for every foot of elevation gained. One scene that I remember with particular fondness is when the region around Mount Hunter suddenly cleared. Mount Hunter (14,570 feet) is one of the most impressive massifs in the world. It is difficult for me to conclude what is more beautiful; viewing Mount Hunter during perfectly clear conditions, or viewing the peak during bizarre, inclement weather. As I laid complacently in my tent during the evening, I watched symmetrical lenticular clouds evolve around the summit of Mount Hunter. Quickly, I set up my camera and photographed the entire peak, the clouds, and an array of other high mountain phenomena associated with the conditions present in the region at that time. As quickly as the clouds developed, however, they dissipated, and with that I zipped myself back inside my tent. Soon after the amazing natural spectacle, I heard a crunching of snow.

"Hello, Ed?"

I unzipped my tent and poked my head out into the whiteout. I looked around into the disorienting blanket of white and picked out a movement of red and blue.

"Hello" I called out.

"Ed!"

"Over here, come on!"

It was Alex, one of the RMI guides I had met at base camp a few days earlier. Once Alex found my exact location, the two of us sat down and discussed the conditions of the region. Although bad, the whiteout was probably not going to last long, at least Alex didn't think so, and I was rightfully inclined to believe his assumption. He had heard over the radio that there was a weak low pressure cell traveling northward from the Gulf of Alaska. So long as it was weak, it was all right, as once it hit land (as it was now doing) it would dissipate. Alex and I talked for about an hour, before his duties as co-leader of a guided expedition called him back. The RMI team had roughly the same itinerary as I did, and we would be near each other throughout the climb. Although I was on a solo expedition, I was glad that I would be near the company of others throughout the trip.

Photograph Page 118:
Camp at the 9,600 Foot Level of the Kahiltna Glacier; #1930
The 9,600 foot level of the Kahiltna Glacier is one of the best spots on Denali to view this huge river of ice. Just beyond this location is Kahiltna Pass, where high winds and dense clouds often funnel through, making this a potentially dangerous area to camp.

Photograph Page 123:
West Ridge of Mount Hunter; #1826
The steep, heavily glaciated west ridge of Mount Hunter has many intricate surface features. Cornices, snow flutes, hanging glaciers, and seracs are just a few of the many intricacies that make this ridge and the countless others like it throughout the Alaska Range so mesmerizing. The scale is daunting as well, from the base of this image to the top of the ridge is a vertical distance of over two thousand feet.

2035   *"Digging Out" in a Snow Storm*

Photograph This Page:
"Digging Out" in a Snow Storm; #2035
Due to the severe climate found in the Alaska Range, climbers are often forced to dig themselves out from huge amounts of snow. "Digging out" was something that I became accustomed to doing frequently while on Denali.

Photograph Page 128:
Mount Hunter Banner Cloud; #2375
This image, taken from the 17,200 foot level of Denali, illustrates the dynamic nature of weather in the Alaska Range. Pictured is a banner cloud, a phenomenon that results from extremely high winds lowering the air pressure on the lee side of a steep mountain slope. Banner clouds appear and then vanish within minutes, granting only brief glimpses of these rare atmospheric formations.

Chapter Twelve

Wind, Cold, and Gravity

2375 *Mount Hunter Banner Cloud*

The next two days were storm ridden and wrought with boredom. During this time, nevertheless, I had a chance to build mental and intestinal fortitude for the days and weeks that lay ahead. I bided my time by eating as much food and getting as much rest as possible. During the second day of the storm, I walked over to where Alex, Ned, and the guided group were camped. I was introduced to everyone, including the lead guide, Paul Meier. Paul had a noticeably raspy voice, an effect of extreme high altitude climbing in the Himalaya just weeks before—he was on an unsuccessful Mount Everest expedition and spent over three weeks above 24,000 feet. I was amazed that he was able to come directly onto a Denali expedition after spending over three months in the Himalaya.

After two days of needed acclimatization, the weather cleared and I packed. Just as I was heading out, I could see Alex, Ned, and Paul with their clients heading toward Kahiltna Pass. The route followed a course up the main Kahiltna Glacier to just below Kahiltna Pass, at an elevation of 10,320 feet. A half hour out of camp, I could see the RMI team rounding the corner which brought them up the slope to the 11,000 foot ice bowl. Kahiltna Pass is a point on Denali where winds funnel through between the north and south side of the mountain, and consequently, conditions can get extremely bad. Although the most recent storm had just passed, there were still clouds which hung above the peaks and ridges of the range. As the day wore on, the clouds dropped and conditions worsened. By the time I reached the spot where I would turn up towards the 11,000 foot bowl, wisps of clouds were streaming through Kahiltna Pass and down the main glacier, straight into my face. I watched as visibility dropped from one hundred percent to about a half mile, then to about a quarter mile. I watched in amazement as large hunks of hoar frost developed on my ladder, ski poles, and backpack. Once in the small valley which led to the ice bowl, however, conditions were milder and visibility increased.

As I neared the ice bowl, I would occasionally look back at the main Kahiltna. A huge stream of a cloud swiftly moved through Kahiltna Pass, and down the main glacier. On the sides of the valley, small lenticulars formed, dissipated, and then reformed. As beautiful as the scene was, however, I knew that what I was witnessing was a prelude to yet another storm. With this in mind, I concentrated on hurrying my pace into camp. The steepness of the glacier, coupled with the debilitating weight I was carrying, and the altitude change, was taking its toll on me. This was the steepest part of the climb thus far, and the ladder was proving awkward. After cresting many glacial undulations and watching the conditions worsen around the ice bowl, I finally caught a glimpse of where I would camp. With this sight, I felt a renewed sense of energy and climbed at full speed ahead. By the time I dropped my pack and sled, every part of my body ached and my muscles trembled with fatigue. As tired as I was, however, I needed to set up camp, quickly.

As I was digging through my gear, Alex came over and offered some hot orange drink. Having someone to talk to relieved the monotony of digging in and erecting my shelter. I crawled into my sleeping bag and ignited my stove just as the first wind driven snow blasted my tent. It was late evening by the time I began eating, and although the conditions were bad outside, I noticed that the clouds would break open periodically and allow the warm hued light from the low Alaskan sun to strike the glaciated landscape. I set up my camera around 10:30 that evening.

For two hours I watched and photographed the surrounding landscape as graceful lenticular clouds formed around the peaks and ridges of the area. The lighting continued to get better, as did the conditions in the ice bowl. Although the skies were clearing around my campsite, the temperature dropped considerably. In order to keep photographing, I set up my stove to periodically warm my hands and avoid numbness, or worse. The low, relatively flat course the Alaskan sun follows results in sunsets that last for hours, and continue to produce increasingly vivid colors right up to when the sun falls below the horizon. As cold as it was, (I later found out that it was twenty below zero that night) the unique conditions kept me from climbing back into my warm sleeping bag.

Throughout my first night at the ice bowl, conditions once again worsened. I awoke the next morning to high winds and one foot of new snow. A peek out of my tent revealed that climbing was definitely not an option. It didn't matter anyway, as I needed to acclimatize before heading up to my next destination at 14,200 feet—a big jump. I spent my day sleeping and cleaning camera equipment and occasionally talking between tent walls to some of the guys from the RMI team. I remembered this spot from the year before. It was the first camp on the mountain where conditions felt really cold. Even during the day, when the storm clouds dissipated to allow the sun to shine, the altitude, subarctic location, and bitter wind made it difficult to function normally.

During dinnertime, I put on my cold weather equipment and emerged from the confines of my tent to talk with the RMI team. It didn't take long for me to feel the conditions, even with thick mittens. I could barely feel my hands. A real problem was created as I started taking pictures of the camp, exposing my raw flesh to the elements. My hands fell instantly numb. Within thirty seconds I had virtually lost all control of both my hands and was fighting to put my camera away and get them into mittens. During my trip, I would constantly be reminded of how brutal an environment Denali really is. As I fought to get my hands into my mittens, the situation turned serious. I had absolutely no control of my fingers and they were turning white. Using my elbows and mouth, I managed to get my left hand covered, then my right. I immediately spun my arms around in an attempt to get blood into my appendages. Slowly, with intense pain, the feeling came back. The pain eventually subsided, replaced by a strange, pervasive itch. From that point on, I made sure that I would never allow any part of me to become exposed as badly as that.

The following day brought similar weather—cold, windy, and low visibility. Although I was acclimatizing, I was eager to get moving. My next goal was to make it to the ice bowl at the 14,200 foot level. This would be a big jump. The previous year, the move from the 11,000 foot bowl to 14,200 feet wasted me, and I was carrying considerably more weight this time. The higher a climber goes, the greater the effect of the given level of ascent becomes. If someone who lives at sea level drives to 4,000 feet, that person will experience very little, if any physiological effects. However, if a climber who is at 8,000 feet ascends 4,000 feet to reach 12,000 feet, there will be significant physiological effects. The fact that I was climbing so far north, where the effects of altitude are increased because the atmosphere is thinner than at more moderate latitudes, forced me to always consider my rate of ascent.

Due to the unpredictability and severity of weather on Alaskan mountains, descending to relieve altitude sickness cannot always be counted on as an option. Although I was eager to get going, I realized I needed to maintain a slow and steady pace. Later in the evening, Alex and I discussed the conditions of the mountain. Judging by the conditions, we both felt that the weather would permit an ascent of Motorcycle Hill the following day.

Sun and sounds of clanking aluminum woke me the next morning. The RMI team was making a carry to the 13,900 foot level.

"Hey Ed! You awake? Wake up!"

It was Alex, and I had slept like a rock for the first time on the trip. I unzipped my tent to see the RMI team in three rope teams moving toward Motorcycle Hill. Because they were moving, Alex and I only exchanged brief morning hellos.

There was a high layer of clouds slightly obscuring the sun, but I was nevertheless blinded by the highly reflective fresh snow. I put my glacier glasses on, surveyed the scene, and decided to make a go for it. The weather was the best it had been since my second day on the mountain, but could easily turn sour.

By 10:00 in the morning, I was packed and ascending the first of Motorcycle Hill. I was wearing snow shoes and had my ladder/sled system rigged up, so climbing was going to be awkward. About one quarter of the way up the slope, at the base of the first big step over an opening crevasse, my left snowshoe came off. Kneeling down with the ladder rigged to me was difficult. I unhooked the whole system, as this was the easiest solution, and secured it to the ground. After lashing the snowshoes to my sled, I continued climbing with just my boots, as the snow surface was hard enough for there not to be any need for snowshoes.

I slowly made my way up the first couple of crevasses. When going over a crevasse that lies on a moderately steep incline, its presence is a bit more obvious than crevasses on leveler ground. There still, however, remain tinges of uncertainty. Instead of the less obvious sag of a snowbridge as is typical of "flat" crevasses, snow bridges over "hill" crevasses reveal their hidden danger by appearing as steps, slightly level at the base, steep over the slot, and level once again at the top. The transitions between these three phases, however, are uncertain. I almost wished that I didn't even know I was traveling over them, as is the case much of the time on the lower, flatter crevasses.

As I got higher on the hill, the grade steepened and I was forced to rest frequently. Hauling over one hundred twenty pounds up this incline at over 11,000 feet was not easy. I began to drop to my knees to rest, panting wildly, and cursing my miserable situation. At one point I looked down to see that my progress was poor at best—after all that work, I was barely half of the way to the top. A little further up from the halfway point, I dropped down once again, this time with feelings of despair. For the first time on the trip, I had thoughts of defeat and retreat. My despair turned to anger, however—anger at the very thought of turning around, something I had never even considered before this point. I cursed my dilemma, and then my ladder. I "unhooked" myself, directly over dangerous crevasse territory and grabbed hold of the front rung of the ladder, and dragged the thing behind me.

"This is stupid!" I thought, the very reason I had the ladder was to protect me from the dangers of terrain I was traveling over. About seventy-five grueling feet further up the hill, the grade lessened and I strapped into the awkward rig once again. After a few more bursts of upward travel, I could see the top of the rise, which ended at a ridge at the base of the true West Buttress. This very sight rejuvenated my motivation to continue onward, and two and a half tough hours after I started up the hill, I unclipped my rig and dropped it, along with my backpack onto level ground, at the top of Motorcycle Hill.

My goal for that day was to go all the way to 14,200 feet, but after that climb, I was so tired, I couldn't think about taking one more step. At the top of the hill, I found a huge "fortress" of a tent shelter right on the crest of the ridge. Nobody was camped there, so I decided to occupy it.

After setting my tent up within the confines of the "Taj McKinley"—the walls of it stood a full two feet higher than my tent—I went out on the corniced ridge and took some photographs of an incredible scene of clouds, snow, far off tundra, and of course, mountains. As intriguing as the clouds were, they spelled the advent of yet another storm. I was now at 11,500 feet on the mountain, camped on the edge of a 5,000 foot drop and completely exposed to extreme winds. I felt secure inside the shelter, however, and since

I didn't have a weather report, I didn't know if these conditions would turn out to be nothing more than a three or four hour storm—or nothing at all.

As the day wore on and the sun got closer o the flat tundra horizon (visible to me only since cresting the ridge), strong winds began coming from the south, bringing small bits of clouds called "scud" along with small amounts of snow. At around midnight, the sun was casting a brilliant orange-red glow on the region. I climbed out of my warm tent with all my camera gear, walked over to some protruding rocks, and took some of the most dramatic photographs I have ever taken.

The wind howled throughout the night, making sleep difficult. I wanted to get to the 14,200 foot bowl the next day and knew that I needed to get a good night's rest. I drifted in and out of sleep until ten o'clock the next morning, when I lethargically dragged myself out of my very comfortable shelter. The weather conditions looked stable, although the wind was still howling. Every so often, the wind blew strong enough to pick up hard ice particles which burned and stung the side of my face. I had to keep every part of my body covered.

I broke camp by noon. The first section of the day's climbing was steep. I was bound for Windy Corner, and was sure that it would live up to its name. For the first time on the climb I strapped on my crampons. The high winds scoured the slopes so thoroughly that they were as hard as solid ice. With an ice ax in one hand, and a telescoping ski pole in the other, I battled both wind and gravity. Every so often, I would look down slope and shudder at the thought of losing my balance—I would almost certainly be dragged off cliff I had camped at the night before. After a couple of very slow hours of climbing, I could see the rocks at the base of Windy Corner. My progress was slow and the winds were accelerating.

It took me a total of five hours just to get to Windy Corner. Once there, I took a quick rest, but was prompted back to my feet as the winds were almost unbearable. A few times, I had to drop to my knees and plant my ice ax in the snow to avoid being blown off balance and tumbling to my death. Once around Windy Corner, however, conditions eased, and I continued along my slow course to the ice bowl. From Windy Corner to the ice bowl, I traversed a moderate slope at the base of the West Buttress. Although I no

Foraker Sunset

2213

longer had the wind to contend with, my progress was hampered by my sled constantly sliding downslope. As I approached my next camp, I maneuvered over a number of glacial irregularities. This was a very disheartening experience, as each time I approached the top of a "hill", I thought I was making my last steps into camp. This must have happened ten times, until I finally crested the last bump and saw a group of tents in the near distance. It took me a half hour to actually reach the ice bowl from there. What a relief it was to take off my ladder rig and prepare for three to five days of rest and acclimatization after climbing twelve hours straight!

Greatly fatigued, I slowly pitched camp. Throughout the day, I had spent as much time as possible observing the weather and cloud formations in the region. Although the sky was obscured by clouds for the better part of the day, it was now clear enough to see the entire range, and for the sun's warming rays to illuminate the surrounding peaks. Looking out toward Mount Foraker, I was instantly motivated to pull out my tripod and set up my camera. Just as a half moon was passing over Mount Foraker's 17,400 foot high summit, a spectacular stack of perfectly shaped lenticular clouds formed to the north of the mountain, and the entire scene was illuminated by the deep crimson of the setting sun. The spectacle was short lived, however. Once the lenticulars dissipated and the lighting faded, I finished setting up camp, ate some food, and fell into deep sleep.

For the next five days I photographed the region, ate as much food as I could stuff into my mouth, and rested for the big move to the high camps. I spent a lot of time talking with the ranger based at the camp, Ron Johnson, who had already been at the 14,200 foot high camp for twenty-four days and would be there for ten more. Ron was responsible for making sure everything went smoothly with the climbers in camp. In the hut he stayed in, there were oxygen tanks, medical emergency supplies, anti-altitude sickness drugs such as Diamox and Decadron, as well as medical diagnostic instruments.

Moonrise over Ridges and Clouds

2323

Denali's weather had been unusually bad in 1991. Many teams descended from the 17,200 foot high camp after being pinned down by extreme weather for two weeks. Luckily, the weather took a turn for the better after I arrived. Due to a very powerful high pressure cell over the Alaska Range, winds died down, and for a few days, the skies were totally cloudless, an event that occurs only about three days per year on the south side of the Alaska Range. After my days of rest, nourishment, and acclimatization at the 14,200 foot camp, I decided to move up to the high camp at 17,200 feet.

On the eve of my ascent of the steep headwall which leads to the top of the West Buttress, I thoroughly prepared my gear. Since I would not be taking my ladder or sled with me, I placed all non-essential equipment in my mule bag, lashed this bag into my sled, and buried it. To mark where my cache was located, I planted my ten foot long aluminum ladder end up—undoubtedly there would be snowfall and I wanted to make sure I would be able to find my supplies after I came back down.

I would take seven days of food and fuel, my climbing and camping hardware, and of course, all my camera equipment, including my tripod. I woke the morning of June twenty-third before the sun had risen over the upper slopes of Denali to the northeast. Conditions were still, and very cold. With my day's goal in mind, I quickly and efficiently packed and dressed. To the west, I could see Mount Foraker in early morning light. To the south, Mount Hunter stood in a cloudless sky, and to the north, stood the 2,000 foot headwall I would be climbing. Once packed, I rechecked everything. At 8:00 in the morning, I bade the ice bowl at 14,200 feet good-bye and headed toward higher ground.

As I walked out of camp, I saw a number of other teams getting ready to move up the headwall as well. The weather was better than anyone had imagined it would be, and nobody wanted to waste any time taking advantage of the opportunity. By 9:30 in the morning, I started ascending the first part of the slope, at 15,000 feet. I soon dropped into the snow to rest and strip off layers, including my storm jacket. The sun was beating down with a vengeance, and heat was much more of a problem than the cold. With each step higher, more of the Alaska Range came into view. Mount Hunter, which dominates the view from base camp, looked much less imposing, as I was now looking down on the mountain!

After resting, I attached my crampons to my boots, secured my belongings, and started up the steepest part of the wall. The climbing was enjoyable and I felt in good health. Because a fall from high on the headwall would spell almost certain disaster, I concentrated on gaining the top of the ridge as quickly as possible. I would rest, climb hard for fifty yards, then rest again. Near the very top of the headwall, the slope steepened further. I had been climbing intensely for three hours with a backpack that weighed sixty-five pounds, and the straps of the pack dug painfully into my shoulders.

One hundred yards from my destination, I went full speed ahead after a good, long rest. I was at 16,000 feet, near the top of Denali's West Buttress—the huge ridge that dominates the western rampart of the mountain—and could now feel the effects of the altitude, cold and wind. The surface of the wall was icy. I made sure that my crampons were firmly planted in the ice before making any moves. The last of the climbing proved to be intense—I had only one ice ax, and was on high, exposed terrain. All of these factors motivated me to move quickly, and I did. By 2:00 in the afternoon, I crested the ridge, and dropped down on the narrow, flat surface.

My goal for the day was to go all the way to the high camp at 17,200 feet, a spot known as the "Crow's Nest". Once on top of the headwall, however, at an elevation of 16,200 feet, my head was pounding and I was taxed from the day's climb. If I stayed at 16,200 feet for a night or two, I would be that much better off once I arrived at the Crow's Nest. This would mean one more camp on the mountain, however, and would deplete a good portion of my food. If I went all the way to 17,200 feet, however, I would risk altitude sickness. Since I was alone, I felt that I had better spend a night acclimatizing at 16,200 feet.

The remainder of the first day at 16,200 was enjoyable. I had the top of the ridge to myself, and spent the day running around shooting images of the mountain range. Although the weather at the start of the day was near perfect, much of the range was shrouded in clouds by evening. I was in one of the worst spots on the mountain if a storm came, and would experience some of the highest winds. I didn't worry too much about this, however, and concentrated on photographing the mountains.

Lying at 63° North Latitude, Denali is the earth's northernmost major mountain. The height, location on earth, great relief, and proximity to the Pacific Ocean's Gulf of Alaska make Denali one of the most brutal regions on the globe. Many climbers who have been to the Himalaya say that Denali is the toughest peak in the world to climb, even those who have been to Mount Everest. Although Denali is 20,320 feet above sea level, atmospheric conditions high on the slopes of this mountain are comparable to those of peaks five thousand feet higher. The reason for this is a phenomena known as the Tropopausal Depression. The lowest layer of the earth's atmosphere is called the Troposphere. The Troposphere is where ninety-nine percent of all weather occurs and where most atmospheric water is found. The layer of air that sits on top of the Troposphere is called the Stratosphere. In between the Troposphere and the Stratosphere is a transitional layer called the Tropopause. The Tropopause is found at approximately 30,000 feet around most of the world. Due to the spin of the earth, however, there is a greater amount of atmosphere at equatorial regions of the globe than at the poles. Due to natural atmospheric cycles and this trend, there is a phenomena known as the Tropopausal Depression, where the thickness of the atmosphere takes a significant "step down" at approximately the 60th parallel. Because the atmosphere is significantly thinner under the depression, humans physiologically respond as if they were two to five thousand feet higher in the Alaska Range for any given altitude, than they would on mountains closer to the equator. The Tropopausal Depression is one more physical phenomenon which makes Denali such a unique and untamed realm.

The next day, the entire region socked in once again. I was forced to sit in my tent and wait out the weather. I hoped that conditions would improve, as I knew that my food was soon going to be in short supply. That second day at 16,200 feet was one of the longest on the entire climb. I could really feel the effects of altitude—laziness, loss of appetite, and occasional dizziness. I knew that once above the 14,000 foot level on Denali, my physical state would weaken, no matter how much food or rest I got. The human body is simply not designed to exist in this type of an environment. I made a decision to go for high camp at 17,200 feet the next day, or descend. This was entirely contingent on the weather. Throughout my restless second night, I continuously opened my tent to peer out at the conditions. Sometimes there would be nothing but wind and white. Other times the clouds would break open, allowing a view of the tremendous sweep of lake speckled tundra to the north, or the ice locked mountains to the south and west. Occasionally, the upper ramparts of Denali to the east would be exposed. I drifted in and out of consciousness throughout the early morning hours, and was finally awakened by the sounds of clanking aluminum and muffled voices. Peering out of my tent, I could see a small group of climbers cresting the ridge. They were a guided group from Alaska Denali Guiding, and rested only briefly near my camp before moving on. I checked out the surrounding weather and decided to hurry up and move to 17,200 feet. There were clouds in the sky and there was about a twenty mile per hour wind, but conditions allowed for a move to the Crow's Nest.

Preparing to make my move to high camp took me much longer than usual. I was weak, and the altitude was having an adverse effect on me. By noon, I was packed and starting the 1,000 foot climb up the ridge. The first section shot directly to the top of a rock outcrop from camp. From there, I wove my way around icy rock, hard snow, and rock outcrops. Halfway up, the ridge became knife-edged, with a 2,500 foot vertical drop to the south and a 7,500 foot drop on the north. In one hand I held an ice ax, in the other, a telescoping ski pole. I used these tools to make sure I didn't tumble off either side of the ridge. I reached a point on the ridge where I could comfortably sit and rest. I looked to the west to see Mount Foraker rising out of a dense river of light gray clouds swiftly flowing from Kahiltna Pass. To the north, large cumulus clouds, fueled by the sun heating the moist tundra, built up along the Alaska Range. I only had another two hundred fifty vertical feet before I arrived at safer ground, and decided to take my time enjoying what must be one of the greatest views in the world.

Although I wasn't as tired as when I woke up, I felt fatigued, and knew that no matter how much food or rest I got, the altitude would ultimately win out. After an extended rest that included shooting photographs of the region, I climbed the last of the ridge and contoured around the south side of a shallow glacial bowl into the Crow's Nest, at 17,200 feet. It had taken me six and a half hours. After dropping my pack, I sat down lethargically, and nursed a pounding headache by massaging my temples. The sun shone brightly, and even with my dark mountaineering glasses on, the intense glare accentuated my head's pain. I was forced to bury my face in my hands. Alex and the RMI crew were camped nearby, but I was too exhausted to give even a brief hello upon arrival.

"You made it."

I looked up to see Alex and Ned.

"How you guys doing?"

"How do you feel, Ed?"

"I...have a bit of a headache...but...I'm...I'm gonna be okay."

The three of us had a limited conversation, but it was definitely nice to see them. After Alex and Ned returned to their camp, I forced myself to set up camp. Since the Crow's Nest is one of the mountain's worst spots to be stuck at during a storm, I dug in good and anchored my little tent solidly. Once finished preparing camp, I walked fifty feet to the south where the small plateau I was camped at dropped off sharply into the ice bowl at 14,200 feet. I stood atop the ice covered rocks which marked the very rim of the ice bowl and peered down three thousand vertical feet, and picked out my ladder. It gave me a strange sense of security, seeing my ladder the better part of a vertical mile below me. I set up my tripod and zoomed in on the summit of Mount Hunter where a dramatic banner cloud streamed from the south side of the peak. After a few hours in the sun, I went back to my camp for the night. Soon after I was in my tent, the sun fell below the West Buttress, shrouding the Crow's Nest in a cold shadow. Soon thereafter, the temperature fell dramatically. I burrowed deeply into my warm shelter, wondering about my chances for a successful summit attempt before falling into sleep.

Photograph Page 135:
Foraker Sunset; #2213
Mount Foraker, 17,400 feet, is the sixth highest mountain in North America. As I arrived at the ice bowl at 14,200 feet of Denali, I watched in amazement as the moon moved over Foraker's summit just as a giant stack of lenticular clouds formed to the north of the peak.

Photograph Page 137:
Moonrise over Ridges and Clouds; #2323
The view from the top of the West Buttress of Denali is incredible. While camped at 16,200 feet on the mountain, I would observe weather conditions change dramatically. One of the most unique views I saw was the moon rising over a carpet of cloud covered ridges.

Helicopter Lifting Supplies from Ranger Camp at 14,200 Feet

Photograph This Page:
Helicopter Lifting Supplies from Ranger Camp at 14,200 Feet ; #2467
The National Park Service maintains an emergency medical camp at the 14,200 foot level of Denali. At the end of the climbing season, this camp is flown out by helicopters. The helicopter shown here is an Aerospatiale Llama, a craft capable of flying to 22,000 feet with a five hundred pound payload.

Photograph Page 144:
Denali North Face Storm; #2665
The north face of Denali is the greatest alpine wall in the world. This huge mountain face rises over 19,000 feet in just eleven miles. This image, taken near Wonder Lake on the low tundra to the north of the mountain, illustrates the scale of the region. The mountains on the bottom of the picture stand 5,000 feet in altitude, while the north summit of Denali, seen here, is 19,470 feet high.

Chapter Thirteen

Whiteout!

2665

Denali North Face Storm

The first night at the Crow's Nest was the coldest yet on the mountain. Any movement inside my thick sleeping bag would "pump" warm air out and suck biting, frigid air in. The conditions were unusually still and quiet, probably the calmest I had yet experienced on the entire climb. Floating in and out of sleep, I amused myself as I watched my breath condense into a thick fog, then fall back onto my face as small particles of ice. The clear, calm conditions allowed the temperature to drop below -40° Fahrenheit, an unbearable temperature in the thin air at 17,000 feet. Although my pounding headache had long since subsided, the extreme cold made deep sleep nearly impossible. The morning's first rays of warming sunlight were a long overdue and very welcome relief.

Shortly after sunrise, I heard the RMI team rustling about and preparing to make a carry to Denali Pass, at 18,200 feet. Alex, Ned, Paul and their clients planned to reach the summit, then descend via the north side of the mountain, and then walk out to Wonder lake on the low tundra to the north of the mountain. Because they would not be descending the same way they climbed, the group had to carry everything, including their sleds. Their carry to Denali Pass would allow them to summit the next day, then descend via Thayer Basin on the north side of the mountain. Before leaving for their day's trip, Alex came over to my camp to find out what my plans were. I was just unzipping my warm sleeping bag (reluctantly) as Alex "knocked" on my tent.

"Hey...Ed"

"What."

Neither of us was very cordial, and I was in a strange state of consciousness.

"What are you doing?"

"Putting on my clothes."

"Oh yeah, can I watch?"

His sarcasm was appreciated and I started laughing, but the thin air only allowed a few seconds of chuckling before I had to force air back into my bloodstream.

"Are you guys going to the summit today?"

"No, we're doing a carry to the pass. Are you going to go?"

I thought about it for a second and decided that I might as well, as the weather was good.

"Well, as soon as I stand up and see how I feel, I'll let you know."

"All right, I guess I'll see you later."

"Okay Alex, good luck."

Alex wished the same to me and was then off. For the next hour, I struggled to get my gear and clothing on. My boots, frozen solid, took fifteen minutes each to slip my feet into. I unzipped the tent and staggered out, noting that my pants were on backwards just as I lost my balance and flopped over in the snow. I decided at that point I would take it easy for the day and remain in camp.

It took me three more hours before I had my act together and was preparing breakfast—fried oatmeal. At high altitudes there is a constant battle against lethargy; throughout the day I wanted to do absolutely nothing. The extent of my activity during the first full day at the Crow's Nest was walking around camp and climbing on nearby rocks. As tired as I was, however, I was able to appreciate the spectacular day. I knew that the conditions would not last for long and made the firm decision to attempt the summit the next day, or descend.

Having been immersed in deep thought for most of the day, I didn't take note of the time, and was surprised when I saw the RMI group coming down from Denali Pass. A glance at my watch revealed that it was late afternoon and I knew that it would be a good idea to start dinner. As soon as the sun set, it would be too cold for any activity short of zipping up my sleeping bag. Just as I was finishing the last of my chili and corn chips (one of the best dinners on the trip), the RMI team staggered into camp. I exchanged a brief wave with the entire team and then retired, knowing full well that the conditions coupled with my apprehension about the next day would allow me only a few hours of sleep, at best.

The morning of the twenty-seventh arrived windy and clear. My tent was almost entirely buried in a snowdrift. Unlike the previous morning, I felt strong and full of energy. I quickly packed my summit necessities (camera, film, food, and water), anchored my tent firmly, and set out. I left my sleeping bag perfectly set up for when I returned, knowing that I would be completely exhausted. My sense of excitement grew as I looked around and saw clear conditions. There were a total of four teams at the Crow's Nest: the RMI team, the Alaska Denali team, a group of Japanese, and me. By 8:00 in the morning, all of us were slowly moving towards Denali Pass.

I contoured around the lower section of the bowl which led to the pass, then stopped to put on my crampons as the wind-scoured surface was hard and icy. Since I was not roped to anyone, I decided to utilize my rest—sprint—rest technique. The higher I got, the stronger I felt, and the longer each sprint became. Near the top of the pass, the slope was steep, almost as steep as the upper section of the headwall on the West Buttress. I put in one good, long rest, drank an energy drink, and took off for my last sprint up to the pass.

"ONE...TWO...THREE...."

I counted out loud with each step.

"TWENTY-FOUR...TWENTY-FIVE...."

I would drive the shaft of my ice ax into the hard snow and pull myself up. It took me forty six steps before the grade finally eased and I could see the actual top of the pass. Without hesitation, I quickly headed straight for a rock outcropping and sat down on top of my backpack. Dizzy with momentary exhaustion, I looked around to see slight wisps of clouds beginning to swirl around the region. Ahead of me were the three Japanese, behind me were the RMI and Alaska-Denali teams. I checked my watch and noted that it only took forty-five minutes to climb 1,000 feet; I was making good time, but I still had over 2,000 vertical feet and quite a bit of distance to go before I was on the top of the continent.

From Denali Pass, I caught my first glimpse of the mountain's summit, far to the southeast. Suddenly, I watched a perfectly clear blue sky turn gray. I had seen the weather turn sour in a matter of minutes in the Alaska Range, but this weather change took place in a matter of *seconds!* I scanned the skies above the summit, which were turning increasingly dark, and noted that cloud base was significantly above the peak. At this point, my anticipation and excitement took over. I decided to press onward. I climbed a series of icy slopes and then traversed the southeast side of an ice bowl that led into a broad plateau—the Football Field. By 11:30 in the morning the summit was engulfed in clouds. My once energetic state was waning. I sat down on a rock outcropping and rested. None of the other climbing teams that had set out for the summit were in sight anymore. The Japanese had sped off toward the summit and the RMI and Alaska-Denali groups had descended. By 11:45 a.m., the cloud that surrounded the summit of Denali was continuing to steadily drop, and was only a few hundred feet above me. I took out my map and noted that I was at the 19,400 foot level—the highest I had ever been. I knew that if I continued on to the summit, I stood a good chance of getting lost and killed, but if I descended I would most likely lack the energy for another summit attempt. I decided to wait five more minutes to see if the conditions would somehow clear. Five minutes went by, and then five more, and then five more after that. By now I was in a solid whiteout and my physical and mental state were significantly impaired. I felt drunk and started hearing voices. At one point I thought I saw my sophomore year roommate, then my mother, hiding behind a rock outcropping. I was losing my mind and had to get down.

Visibility was only about ten yards, forcing me to follow my crampon tracks for visual bearing. My sullen feeling of defeat was quickly replaced by the urgency of survival. The visibility would vary from only a couple of feet to as much as twenty-five yards, and the winds were gaining strength. One of the effects of altitude is a condition called ataxia, or loss of balance. I found myself stumbling around. My loss of balance caused me to trip and fall a half dozen times. At one point, I was forced to crawl with my face only a few inches above the surface of the snow to find my way. Throughout my descent, the squeal of the crampons in the snow made me think there were people behind me. Many times I would stop, turn around, and yell to see if there was anyone around, but there never was. The whiteout was hell. I couldn't see where I was going, nor where I had come from. Everywhere I looked, I would see nothing but blinding white. Three hours after I had set out from my high point, I recognized that I was only five hundred feet above Denali Pass. Once again, I thought I heard voices, but brushed it off as my mind playing tricks on me. I was both startled and relieved, however, when I turned around to see two faces appear out of the white.

"HELLO!" I yelled.

"HELLO!"

It was the Japanese team. I stopped and greeted them once again.

"There are only two of you, where is the third?" I was worried that something had happened.

"He is on the summit. He is waiting for the conditions to clear."

"Why is he waiting for the conditions to clear up?"

"He is going to paraglide off the summit."

I couldn't believe what I was hearing, but was too worried about my own well being to be worried about someone waiting out a storm on the summit of Denali. The three of us descended together, and were relieved that the lower we got, the greater the visibility became. I quickly down-climbed the icy slopes to Denali Pass and sat down to rest, awaiting the arrival of the Japanese. Once we were together, I gave my two friends some water, and they gave me some dried fish. To my disbelief, the two pulled out a pack of cigarettes and lit up—at 18,200 feet above sea level—in the middle of a storm!

From the top of Denali Pass, I could vaguely make out the Crow's Nest, and started down the slope just as the Japanese were finishing their cigarette. The top of the descent was a true "white knuckle" adventure. One slip would prove disastrous. I concentrated acutely and moved quickly with calculated steps. It only took twenty-five minutes for me to descend the slope and another ten to reach camp. As I walked by the RMI tents, Alex popped his head out and greeted me with relief.

"Man, I thought we were going to have to get a rescue team after you."

"Thanks for worrying, but everything's all right."

"How far did you make it?"

"Football Field. I rested there, then decided to return. How far did you guys make it?"

"We didn't go much past Denali Pass. The cloud was dropping way too fast for us. That's when we turned back, so did the Alaska-Denali team."

"Well, I'm starving and exhausted. I'll talk to you later."

I walked the remaining distance to my tent and found it buried by drifted snow.

It wasn't long before I had my shelter dug out and was inside my sleeping bag. For the next three hours I stared at the tent walls and thought about being so close to my goal. In only a matter of minutes, my chance for a successful summit day was swallowed up by a dense cloud. I thought about the long journey back to base camp I would have to endure. I had a long way to go, and could only descend when the weather would let me, which might not be for a long time. Over dinner, I reevaluated my situation and decided that if conditions cleared, I would make one more summit attempt. I dug through my food and realized that I would have to strictly ration my supplies. For the next twelve hours, I sat still inside my shelter, sometimes sleeping, sometimes reflecting on my Denali experiences so far, sometimes thinking of the future, both near and distant. For the first time, I realized how much energy and time I had devoted to traveling to this peak and trying to climb it. It had been a dream of mine since early childhood, and I had just been within 1,000 feet of the summit. By the time the first rays of sunlight struck my tent the next morning, I had decided that I would not leave without getting to the top of the mountain. Even if I had to scrounge food and fuel from other expeditions on the mountain, I would keep trying.

Although my first summit attempt had almost taxed all my energy, I felt good on the morning of the twenty-eighth. The whiteout was now replaced by extreme winds, keeping everyone at the Crow's Nest pinned in camp. I stuck my head out and watched powerful, turbulent gusts of wind swirl snow and ice down the slopes of Denali Pass. These periodic gusts would tear through camp and nearly flatten everyone's tents. Around noon, while digging my tent out, I looked up to the top of Denali Pass to see a lone figure stagger down the steep slope. It was the Japanese climber who had planned to paraglide off the summit. Everyone at high camp watched as the poor guy got knocked over by the high winds and then struggled to his feet only to be blown over once again. It took him over an hour to descend. It's hard to believe that he was even able to made it down.

For the remainder of the day, I bided my time by eating and drinking as much as I could. As sunset neared, the winds abated and the sky was remarkably clear. To the north, I could see a 737 flying around the mountain, a rare treat for passengers. It was the first time I actually looked down on a jet liner! I walked over to the RMI team and we all agreed to keep our fingers crossed for the weather to hold out for the next day. At 8:00 p.m. I followed Paul over to the rocks at the edge of the Crow's Nest and listened to the weather forecast that Annie was transmitting. It was good news—a high pressure cell was moving over the region and would stay for the next few days. This explained the high winds, as the air from the high pressure cell rushed down to the low pressure cell. For a season wrought with terrible weather, it seemed that I was at the right place at just the right time.

"Well, Ed, looks like you're going to get another chance to kill yourself."

I laughed at Paul's sarcasm.

"Well, I'll see you on top tomorrow."

"Good luck."

"Thanks. Good luck to you."

I walked off to my tent just as a tremendous avalanche broke away from near the top of one of the Kahiltna Peaks and roared down into the northeast fork of the Kahiltna Glacier. It was a chilling reminder of how deadly the region can be.

Photograph Page 152:
Denali Reflection; #2594
Denali is the greatest mountain in the world in terms of vertical relief. The peak rises 19,000 feet in only eleven miles. The impressive north side of Denali is rarely seen in its entirety, as storms often shroud its slopes.

Chapter Fourteen

The Final Steps

2594

Denali Reflection

I awoke the morning of June twenty-ninth after a good, solid sleep. After packing, I looked out over the Kahiltna region and the whole of the Alaska Range. Unbelievably, I could make out the Gulf of Alaska, one hundred fifty miles to the south. If I was going to make it, this was the day. I double checked my gear and food (the last morsels I had left), put on my crampons, and then set out for Denali Pass. The Alaska Denali and the RMI teams were ahead of me, but in my excitement, I quickly caught up and passed two of their rope teams. It took little more than half an hour for me to reach the pass. I was climbing faster than before. At the top of the pass, I once again saw my goal, this time with a crystal-clear blue sky as a backdrop. I used my rest—sprint—rest—sprint technique up the ice slopes above Denali Pass. At one point, I was so exhausted that I collapsed, almost losing my bladder. Two hours after reaching Denali Pass, I passed my previous high point and enjoyed the level topography of the Football Field. For the better part of the day, my pace was equal to that of the RMI team, but much slower than the Alaska Denali group. Just as I was halfway across the Football Field, the guys from Alaska-Denali were coming down and passed me by. It was encouraging to see that there was already a summit victory for the day.

By 4:00 in the afternoon, I was at the base of the summit ridge of Denali. I dropped my backpack and secured it with one of my ski poles, and took only the bare essentials for the summit. Using my ice ax, one ski pole, and my crampons, I slowly climbed the crevassed and very icy slope to the crest of the summit ridge. Each step was exhilarating. Out of anticipation, I would break out of my pace and sprint ahead. I would soon collapse, however, in the thin air. By 5:00 in the evening, I was at the crest of the summit ridge. Just three hundred vertical feet and a precarious five hundred yard traverse to the east was the highest point on the continent. I rested on the summit ridge as the RMI team passed by. We all smiled at each other. I was going to make it, there was no doubt about it, just three hundred feet higher. I took out my camera and carefully photographed the region with an assortment of lenses. Utilizing my ski pole as a makeshift monopod, I photographed the RMI guys maneuvering around a giant cornice on their way to the summit. After shooting two rolls of film, I packed, and took the first of my last steps to Denali's summit. The climb was precarious. To my left, there was a five hundred foot drop into the Football Field, and to my right, there was a ten thousand foot vertical drop down the South Face. I was amazed to find a small square hole, barely large enough for a person to fit into, where the Japanese would-be paraglider pilot had slept for the night. I carefully coordinated each footstep, one by one, and took heed to stay below the fracture line of any cornices.

The ridge seemed to go on forever. I could feel my heart pounding out of exertion and exhilaration. After rounding a huge cornice, I could see the RMI group crowded on a patch of snow with no land higher, anywhere. Twenty more panting steps brought me next to Paul, standing on the highest point of North America, the summit of Denali—20,320 feet, 6194 meters above sea level. I looked at my watch. It was 5:29 p.m.

"Congratulations Ed, twenty years old and you solo climbed Denali."

"Thanks, Paul, but I guess the fact that I'm shaking your hand means that I didn't really solo."

"Sure you did. You weren't roped to anyone this whole time and didn't receive any help from anyone. You did it on your own."

I waited until all the RMI team members had their pictures taken and were descending, then took my own self portraits on the top. I think that I was more excited about the views than anything else. I spent only fifteen minutes alone on top, enjoying the view, taking pictures, and relaxing. I scratched my name into the snow with the tip of my ice ax, took one last panoramic view of the region, and started down. Most mountaineering accidents occur during the descent, when climbers are more relaxed and fatigued. I forced myself to concentrate heavily on making only calculated, well placed movements. I worked my way down the ridge, took one last view south from the crest, then descended to the Football Field.

Although the weather conditions were great for a summit day, I wanted to be back at the Crow's Nest before sunset. After collecting my belongings at the base of the summit ridge, I marched double time across the Football Field. I felt like one big wet noodle. My muscles were so fatigued, but I was more secure both physically and mentally with each step lower in altitude. My thoughts while descending were strange, and very difficult to relate. I would feel that my success was no big deal, forget what I had even done, then be struck with elation on having summitted. More than once on my descent

A long way from my childhood trash can, 6194 meters above sea level
—on the summit of Denali

I caught myself smiling. By 8:00, I had reached Denali Pass, where I met Alex (who had descended earlier with a sick climber) and one of the guides from the Alaska Denali group, Randy, who had to descend with a sick client as well. Spontaneously, Alex and I gave each other a bear hug and Alex yelled at the top of his lungs.

"YOU MADE IT! YOU BASTARD, YOU MADE IT!"

"What the hell you two doing now?" I couldn't understand why the two of them were going up just before sunset.

"We're going for a midnight summit!"

Our meeting was short, but uplifting. I wished Alex and Randy good luck, and then descended to my high camp. I arrived at my tent just as the sun was setting. I ate the very last crumbs of my food and collapsed into my sleeping bag. I had been climbing for over twelve hours—from 17,200 feet to 20,320 feet, and then back down, and was totally exhausted. I had some very bizarre dreams that night, none of which I can remember, but they were definitely exhaustion-induced.

I groggily awoke the day of my descent around 10:00 a.m. It wasn't until noon that I started making my way down the ridge toward 16,000 feet. On my descent, I watched some of the most spectacular cumulonimbus (thunderhead) clouds form on the northern margin of Denali. By the time I was going down the headwall into the 14,200 foot bowl, these clouds had spilled into the region and were blocking the sun. I passed a number of teams climbing the headwall, hoping to take advantage of the good but deteriorating weather, and felt great, knowing that I had behind me what they were going to have to endure. As good as it was being up so high, I was exhausted and starved, and wanted to get back to sea level. By late afternoon, I was digging out my sled at the ice bowl, and brewing up a huge dinner. Compared to the Crow's Nest, the ice bowl at 14,200 feet was balmy, and the change in altitude made a world of physiological difference. After eating and setting up camp, I walked over to the ranger hut where Ron was stationed and got the weather report— rapidly worsening. I had definitely lucked-out with the weather. I planned to reach base camp the following day. I knew that the condition of the lower glacier would be atrocious. Because the few snowbridges that remained would be very weak, and even more so during the heat of the mid-day sun, I would have to travel over the lower glacier during the early morning hours.

Around noon on July first, I harnessed into my crevasse ladder, and began my long descent to base camp. Although I started out in relatively warm conditions, a partial whiteout soon enveloped the area. Step by step, I made my way to Windy Corner, jumping two crevasses, and nearly getting buried by a small avalanche that ended only a few hundred feet above me. By 4:00 in the afternoon, the whiteout had worsened, and my descent was complicated further by an uncooperative sled. Because I was descending, I was forced to reverse the position of the sled relative to my body. I moved it from behind me to in front of me. The wet condition of the snow made the sled stick, but once jarred into movement, it didn't want to stop. The descent from Windy Corner to the top of the 11,000 foot ice bowl proved to be one of the most difficult trials of the entire climb. Due to the grade of the slope, I was constantly in danger of being dragged down the mountain by an out of control sled. At one point, I was forced to unclip from my ladder and crawl

The Alaska Range from the Summit of Denali

2443

with the entire rig in front of me. Once, I nearly lost all my gear as the sled and ladder started sliding away from me into the white abyss. I was barely able to thrust my ice ax in front of the last rung of the ladder, stopping all of my gear (including camera and film) from careening into the Peter's Basin. By the time I reached the top of the 11,000 foot ice bowl, I felt completely defeated by the mountain, but had no choice but to continue.

The descent into the ice bowl proved extremely demanding, but not nearly as difficult as what I had just done. I came to two large crevasses that I needed to cross. Both were too wide to jump, so I laid the ladder over each one of them and walked across. Ten hours after leaving the 14,200 foot level, I was at the 11,000 foot ice bowl. After resting for about a half hour, I set out once again. I quickly maneuvered through the giant glacial hummocks that led to Kahiltna Pass and then onto the main Kahiltna Glacier. The stretch from Kahiltna Pass to base camp was the loneliest of the whole climb. The solitude, however, was fitting for the end of my solo adventure. The condition of the lower Kahiltna was even worse than I had thought it would be. Although my feet were throbbing with pain, I forced myself to march as fast as I could without rest. The ash layer laid down from the 1989 Mount Redoubt eruption was exposed, lowering the albedo (reflectance), and increasing the rate of melt and deterioration of the glacial surface and snowbridges.

Around midnight, I passed by the northeast fork of the main Kahiltna and was shocked by the state of the glacier. For the next three hours, I slogged through a frightening jumble of broken glacial debris and collapsed snowbridges. I navigated around crevasses that three weeks earlier I never knew existed, crevasses that could swallow an entire rope team, let alone my relatively tiny crevasse ladder.

By 3:00 in the morning of July second, I was struggling up the southeast fork, or "Heartbreak Hill". I felt an increasingly greater sense of relief the closer I got to base camp. Finally, at 3:15 in the morning, I dropped my rig down next to the base camp hut, and collapsed on my mule bag. I had successfully solo climbed Denali and come back safely.

The next day arrived with mildly stormy weather. The RMI group came in around 9:00 in the morning and we all celebrated together with cheese covered nachos and jalapenos. Annie called Dave Lee on the radio telephone, and I had nothing more to do but wait. A couple hours later, I heard the loud buzz of Dave's 185 and spotted the small craft against the southeast ridge of Mount Foraker. An hour later, I was back at Talkeetna, nursing my battered feet, drinking beer, and stuffing my face with food. After checking in with the rangers, I began a three day session of celebration and physical recovery with the other climbers in town. When the celebrations finally ended, I worked off my flight with Dave and then headed out to explore and photograph other parts of wild Alaska.

Photograph Page 157:
The Alaska Range from the Summit of Denali; #2443
The view from the Summit of Denali is truly incredible. On a clear day, the visibility can exceed one hundred fifty miles. The view shown here is to the south of the peak: the prominent mountain in the middle is Mount Hunter, 14,570 feet, to the left of Hunter is Mount Huntington, 12,240 feet. The prominent ridge that runs from the lower left of the image is the South Buttress of Denali. On the lower right of the image is Mount Francis, 10,450 feet, and just below Francis, to the left, is base camp, 7,200 feet. The Kahiltna Glacier sits prominently to the right of Mount Hunter and base camp. To the left of Mount Huntington lies the Ruth Glacier and the Ruth Amphitheater.

Map Pages 160 & 161:
Denali & Kahiltna Region, showing West Buttress Climbing Route
This map, created from USGS topographical sheets Talkeetna D-3 and Mt. McKinley A-3, details the West Buttress climbing route. The scale is 1:63,360 (1 inch = 1 mile), and the contour interval is 500 feet. This map is available as a separate item from Ed Darack Photography, stock #MP-1

159

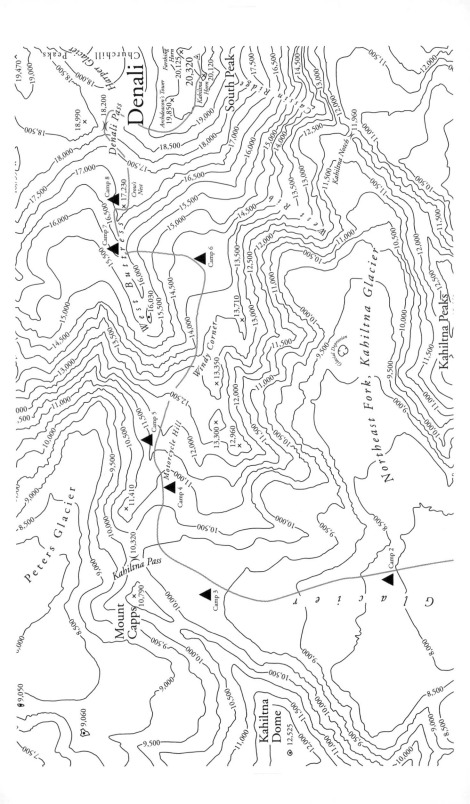

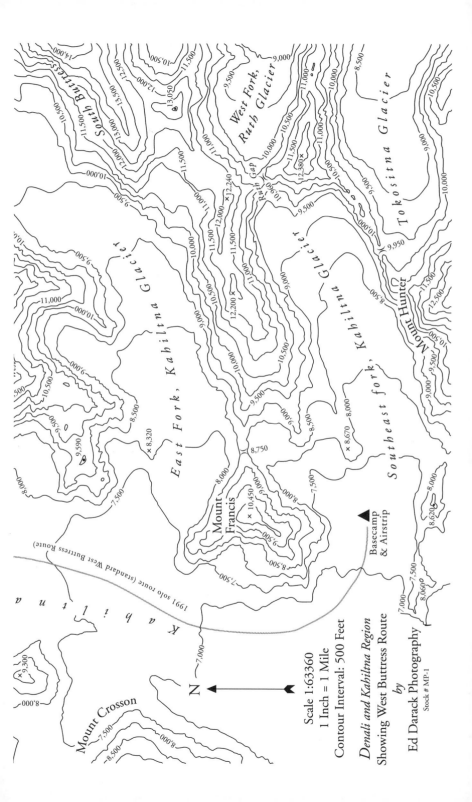

Scale 1:63360
1 Inch = 1 Mile
Contour Interval: 500 Feet

Denali and Kabiltna Region
Showing West Buttress Route
by
Ed Darack Photography

Stock # MP-1

Cover and Page 3: Image #2051; *Storm Over Kahiltna Region;* 1991
Nikon Fm2 • 28mm Nikkor lens • Tripod • 1/60 sec @ f/16 on Kodachrome 64.
Title and Page 128: Image #2375; *Mount Hunter Banner Cloud;* 1991
Nikon Fm2 • 70-210mm zoom lens @ 180mm • Tripod • 1/60 sec @ f/8 on Kodachrome 64.
Copyright and Page 135: Image #2213; *Mount Foraker Sunset;* 1991
Nikon Fm2 • 70-210mm zoom lens @ 180mm • Tripod • 1/15 sec @ f/8 on Kodachrome 64.
Page 4: Image #1815; *Airplane under Mount Hunter;* 1991
Nikon Fm2 • 70-210mm zoom lens @ 135mm • Tripod • 1/15 sec @ f/11 on Kodachrome 25.
Page 6 and Rear Cover: Image #1716; *Denali from the Air;* 1991
Nikon Fm2 • 50mm lens with polarizer • 1/60 sec @ f/5.6 on Kodachrome 64.
Page 9: Image #1999; *Clouds and Kahiltna Region;* 1991
Nikon Fm2 • 70-210mm zoom lens @ 135mm • Tripod • 1/15 sec @ f/8 on Kodachrome 64.
Page 10: Image #1479; *Sunrise on East Face of Mount Whitney;* 1991
Nikon Fm2 • 70-210mm zoom lens @ 135mm • Tripod • 1/15 sec @ f/8 on Kodachrome 64.
Page 27: Image #1658; *Glacier from Air;* 1991
Nikon Fm2 • 50mm lens with polarizer • 1/125 sec @ f/8 on Kodachrome 64.
Page 28: Image #16686; *Moonlight on Mount Shasta;* 1993
Nikon Fm2 • 35mm lens • Tripod • 20 minute exposure @ f/4 on Fujichrome Velvia.
Page 35: Image #1788; *South Face of Denali;* 1991
Nikon Fm2 • 70-210mm zoom lens @ 135mm w/ polarizer • Tripod • 1/125 sec @ f/8 on KR64.
Page 36: Image #1700; *Kahiltna Region from Air;* 1991
Nikon Fm2 • 50mm lens with polarizer • 1/60 sec @ f/5.6 on Kodachrome 64.
Page 44: Image #1749; *Clouds Shrouding Summit of Mount Crosson;* 1991
Nikon Fm2 • 70-210mm zoom lens @ 210mm w/ polarizer • Tripod • 1/125 sec @ f/8 on KR64.
Page 45: Image #1901; *Crevasse Field and Ridge;* 1991
Nikon Fm2 • 70-210mm zoom lens @ 135mm • Tripod • 1/60 sec @ f/8 on KR 64.
Page 46: Image #1647; *Susitna River from Air;* 1991
Nikon Fm2 • 50mm lens with polarizer • 1/125 sec @ f/8 on Kodachrome 64.
Page 61: Image #2844; *Caribou Grazing under Denali;* 1991
Nikon Fm2 • 50mm lens with polarizer • 1/60 sec @ f/5.6 on Kodachrome 64.
Page 62: Image #1679; *Lower Kahiltna Glacier through Cumulus;* 1991
Nikon Fm2 • 50mm lens with polarizer • 1/60 sec @ f/5.6 on Kodachrome 64.
Page 66: Image #1821; *Corniced and Fluted Ridges at Sunset;* 1991
Nikon Fm2 • 70-210mm zoom lens @ 135mm w/ polarizer • Tripod • 1/125 sec @ f/8 on KR64.
Page 67: Image #1806; *Mount Hunter;* 1991
Nikon Fm2 • 50mm lens with polarizer • Tripod • 1/60 sec @ f/5.6 on Kodachrome 64.
Page 72: Image #1718; *Crevasse Field from Air;* 1991
Nikon Fm2 • 50mm lens with polarizer • 1/125 sec @ f/8 on Kodachrome 64.
Page 79: Image #135; *Climbers under Denali;* 1990
Minolta X-370 • 28-105mm zoom lens @ 28mm • 1/60 sec @ f/4 on Kodachrome 64.
Page 84: Image #1993; *Ridges and Cornices at Sunset;* 1991
Nikon Fm2 • 70-210mm zoom lens @ 180mm • Tripod • 1/15 sec @ f/8 on Kodachrome 64.

Page 88: Image #171; *View from inside Crevasse;* 1990
Minolta X-370 • 50mm lens • exposure unrecorded • Kodachrome 64.

Page 92: Image #805; *La Malinche and El Pico de Orizaba;* 1990
Minolta X-370 • 50mm lens • exposure unrecorded • Kodachrome 64.

Page 96: Image #765; *Iztaccihuatl from Popocatepetl;* 1990
Minolta X-370 • 50mm lens • exposure unrecorded • Kodachrome 64.

Page 97: Image #826; *Popocatepetl;* 1990
Minolta X-370 • 50mm lens • exposure unrecorded • Kodachrome 64.

Page 105: Image #14891; *Saint Elias Mountains from the Air;* 1993
Nikon Fe2 • 50mm lens w/ polarizer • 1/500 sec @ f/8 on Fujichrome Velvia.

Page 106: Image #1859; *Preparing to Leave Base Camp;* 1991
Nikon Fm2 • 50mm lens • Kodachrome 64.

Page 112: Image #2091; *Clouds above McKinley River at Sunset;* 1991
Nikon Fm2 • 50mm lens • Tripod • 1/60 sec @ f/11 on Kodachrome 64.

Page 115: Image #1661; *Tundra and Rivers below Clouds;* 1991
Nikon Fm2 • 50mm lens w/ polarizer • 1/125 sec @ f/8 on Kodachrome 64.

Page 118: Image # 1930; *Camp at 9,600 feet;* 1991
Nikon Fm2 • 50mm lens • 1/125 sec @ f/8 on Kodachrome 64.

Page 120: Image #1881; *Snowshoeing up Main Kahiltna Glacier;* 1991
Nikon Fm2 • 50mm lens w/ polarizer • esxposure unrecorded • Kodachrome 64.

Page 123: Image #1826; *West Ridge of Mount Hunter;* 1991
Nikon Fm2 • 70-210mm zoom lens @ 180mm • Tripod • 1/15 sec @ f/8 on Kodachrome 64.

Page 127: Image #2035; *"Digging Out";* 1991
Nikon Fm2 • 50mm lens • esxposure unrecorded • Kodachrome 64.

Page 137: Image #2323; *Moonrise over Ridges and Clouds;* 1991
Nikon Fm2 • 28mm lens • Tripod • 1/60 sec @ f/8 on Kodachrome 64

Page 143: Image #2467; *Helicopter;* 1991
Nikon Fm2 • 50mm lens • exposure unrecorded • Kodachrome 64.

Page 144: Image #2665; *Denali North Face Storm;* 1991
Nikon Fm2 • 70-210mm zoom lens w/polarizer @ 180mm • Tripod • 1/15 sec @ f/8 on KR 64.

Pages 152 and 168: Image #2594; *Denali Reflection;* 1991
Nikon Fm2 • 28mm lens • 1/125 sec @ f/11 on Kodachrome 64.

Page 157: Image #2443; *The Alaska Range from Summit of Denali;* 1991
Nikon Fm2 • 50mm lens w/ polarizer • Monopod • 1/125 sec @ f/8 on Kodachrome 64.

Page 165: Image #2009; *Lenticular Cloud over Mount Capps;* 1991
Nikon Fm2 • 70-210mm zoom lens @ 180mm • Tripod • 1/15 sec @ f/8 on KR 64.

6194 Denali Solo was created in Davis, California by Ed Darack Photography. The text of the book was written in Microsoft Word version 5.1 and imported into Aldus Pagemaker version 5.0 for page layout. The typeface used is Adobe Garamond, set at a point size of 10.5 with a leading of 14 points (10.5 on 14). All images were duplicated from their original 35 millimeter color format to 4 by 5 inch black and white internegatives, enlarged to 5 by 7 inch glossy prints, and then cropped to book proportions. The photographs were scanned on a high resolution flatbed scanner, converted to grey-scale encapsulated Postscript files (EPS), scaled, and dropped into the Pagemaker files.

The Denali map (available from Ed Darack Photography as a separate item) was created by taking two USGS 1:63,360 topographical sheets (Talkeetna D-3 and Mt. McKinley A-3), scanning them at 280 dots per inch resolution, importing them into Aldus Freehand, then tracing each 500 foot contour interval with the freehand pen tool. Certain pieces of information were added and some were left out to fit the specific purpose of the map. The final map was exported to Pagemaker as an encapsulated Postscript file (EPS). The computer platform used was the Apple Macintosh Classic II, running system 7.1. The computer files were output directly from disk to film on a 2,540 dpi imagesetter after being impositioned onto 8-up signatures with impostrip software. Halftones were manually stripped in. All presswork was done by Gilliland Printing Company in Arkansas City, Kansas on a sheet feed press. The cover is printed on 12 point coated one side paper and the text is printed on high opaque 60 pound text. The cover image (available as an 18 by 26 inch lithograph) was printed as a duotone.

I am indebted to a number of people for their help and encouragment.

Thank you to my mother, Judy Darack

Mark Lange, Amy Esterle, Tracy Tingle, Skip Jacobs, Dave and Julie Lee and all those at Talkeetna Air Taxi, Alex, Ned, Paul and the rest of the 1991 RMI Meier team, Bill Debruhl, Jack Ives, Nigel Allan, UC Davis Geography Department, Gilliland Printing, David Gaskill, Graphic Gold, The Printer, Josh Glaser, Doug Van Lare, Steve Stevenson, Galen Rowell, Elliot Welch, Mark Vogel, Nathan Bachtell, Damon Nelson, Todd McHenry, Mike Kay, The Adventurers Club, The Explorers Club, Jake Palmer and family, Terry Tafoya, Cliff Feldheim, Mark Axen, Ron Johnson, Ed Ross, John Dawkins, Bill Winternitz and Doctors at Davis Orthopedic.

2009   *Lenticular Cloud over Mount Capps*

Photograph This Page:

LenticularCloud over Mount Capps; #2009
The Kahiltna region is not only a realm of amazing landscapes, but of surreal displays of weather. One of the most graceful examples is the lenticular cloud, seen here above Mount Capps.

Photograph of Ed Darack by Amy Esterle

Ed Darack is a professional outdoor photographer and writer who resides in Davis, California. He travels extensively around the globe seeking the wildest places the natural world has to offer and captures these regions on film. His award winning images are seen worldwide in books magazines, and galleries.

Ed received a Bachelor of Science degree in the field of Physical Geography from the University of California at Davis and extensively uses the knowledge gained from this curriculum in his profession. His company, Ed Darack Photography, apart from supplying stock images worldwide, publishes lines of notecards, posters, calendars, books, maps, guides, photographic instructional booklets, and an assortment of other paper products. Products by Ed Darack Photography are of the highest quality, as Ed himself is active in every aspect of the publishing process, from the initial image, to the thoughtful descriptions, layouts, maps, and diagrams featured in his companies' merchandise. Ask for products by Ed Darack Photography at quality bookstores, card and gift shops, and outdoor oriented retail outlets near you. In addition to publishing, Ed lectures and gives slide shows across North America. For more information on products, lecture / slide show bookings, or to receive a catalogue, please write, call, or fax:

Ed Darack Photography
Post Office Box 2091
Davis, CA 95617

Toll Free Phone / Fax Order Line:
800.355.5294

Ed Darack Photography is a publisher of a wide range of fine paper products. The images featured in 6194 *Denali Solo* are available as notecards and photographic prints, including the cover image, *Storm over Kahiltna Region,* which is also available as an 18 by 26 inch signed lithograph. A catalog number is located along the lower left side of each image for order identification. Please note that with the exception of *Storm over Kahiltna Region,* all notecards are in color; prints can be ordered either as color or black and white (the original images were made with color slide film). Please write to the address below for a free catalogue and order form, or fill out the condensed form below of popular Ed Darack Photography products.

Photographic prints are available in three sizes, 8 by 10 inch, 11 by 14 inch, and 16 by 20 inch. All are hand printed and come matted and signed; the 8 by 10 and 11 by 14 are unlimited in issue and the 16 by 20 inch format are available limited and unlimited. The cost of an 8 by 10 inch print is $35.00, an 11 by 14 is $60.00, and a 16 by 20 inch print is $200.00; please write to Ed Darack Photography for updated pricing of specific images. To order a print, please indicate image number, title, and the size.

— — — — — — — — (Photocopy or cut out and send or fax in) — — — — — — — —

Stock #	Description	Quantity	Item Price	Item Total
BK-1	6194 *Denali Solo*		$12.00	
PR-2051	*Storm Over Kahiltna Region* Signed Lithograph		$15.00	
NC-2051	*Storm Over Kahiltna Region* Notecard		$2.00	
NC-(Image#)	Notecard with specified image		$2.00	
NS-1	6194 *Denali Solo* notecard set 12 different images from book		$20.00	
MP-1	Denali Map, featured in book		$5.00	

Please add $2.00 per book ordered, $1.00 per dozen cards, 2.50 per poster or map, and 7.50 per photographic print for shipping and handling.

Subtotal	
Applicable Tax	
Shipping and Handling	
Total	

Please include check or money order (Payable in U.S. funds) to:
Ed Darack Photography • PO Box 2091 • Davis • CA • 95617
For additional product information, call or fax toll free: **800.355.5294**

Name.......................................—————————————————

Address....................................—————————————————

City, State, Zip / Postal Code......—————————————————

Country...................................—————————————————

Phone #..................................—————————————————

Denali Reflection

Photograph This Page:
Denali Reflection; #2594
This image displays the great north wall of Denali and its reflection in a tundra pond, in the vicinity of Wonder Lake. To the north of the mountain lies a spectacular sweep of pond and lake speckled tundra. Denali is rarely visible in its entirety; soon after this image was made, the view was obscured by clouds.

Back Cover Photograph:
Denali from Air; #1716
This image, of the seldom seen southwest side of Denali, was taken from an airplane while flying into base camp (out of picture). The west Buttress can be seen to the left of the cloud obscured summit.